Building Dreamweaver® 4 and Dreamweaver® UltraDev™ 4 Extensions

Building Dreamweaver® 4 and Dreamweaver® UltraDev™ 4 Extensions

Tom Muck
Ray West

Osborne/**McGraw-Hill**

New York Chicago San Francisco
Lisbon London Madrid Mexico City
Milan New Delhi San Juan
Seoul Singapore Sydney Toronto

Osborne/McGraw-Hill
2600 Tenth Street
Berkeley, California 94710
U.S.A.

To arrange bulk purchase discounts for sales promotions, premiums, or fund-raisers, please contact Osborne/**McGraw-Hill** at the above address. For information on translations or book distributors outside the U.S.A., please see the International Contact Information page immediately following the index of this book.

Building Dreamweaver® 4 and Dreamweaver® Ultradev™ 4 Extensions

1234567890 FGR FGR 01987654321

ISBN 0-07-219156-2

Publisher	Brandon A. Nordin
Vice President & Associate Publisher	Scott Rogers
Acquisitions Editor	Jim Schachterle
Project Editor	Jennifer Malnick
Acquisitions Coordinator	Timothy Madrid
Technical Editor	Massimo Foti
Copy Editor	Sally Engelfried
Proofreader	Marian Selig
Indexer	Claire Splan
Computer Designer	Roberta Steele
Illustrator	Alex Putney
Series Designer	Roberta Steele
Cover Series Design	Greg Scott
Cover Illustration	Eliot Bergman
Series Illustrator	Lyssa Sieben-Wald

This book was composed with Corel VENTURA™ Publisher.

About the Authors

Tom Muck is coauthor of two other UltraDev books, including the bestseller *Dreamweaver UltraDev4: The Complete Reference*. He is an extensibility expert focused on the integration of Macromedia products with ColdFusion and other languages, applications, and technologies. Tom has been recognized for this expertise as the 2000 recipient of Macromedia's Best UltraDev Extension Award; he also authors articles and speaks at conferences on this and related subjects. As Senior Applications Developer for Integram in Northern Virginia, Tom develops back-end applications for expedited, electronic communications. He runs the Basic-UltraDev site with coauthor Ray West.

Ray West is the Vice President and CIO of Workable Solutions, Inc., an Orlando-based company specializing in the Web-based administration of health care alliances. He has been building data driven Web applications since 1995 including work for HBO, NBC, and *USAToday*, and is coauthor of the best-selling book *Dreamweaver UltraDev 4: The Complete Reference*. Ray lives in Orlando with his wife and son.

Contents at a Glance

Contents

Acknowledgments

Tom's Acknowledgements

This is our second book. After the first monster book (*Dreamweaver UltraDev 4: The Complete Reference*, also published by Osborne/McGraw-Hill), writing this book was like taking a much-needed break. Extensions are one of my passions, so writing a book about extensions was like getting paid for what I like to do—create extensions for Dreamweaver and UltraDev. I couldn't have done it without the help of several people, though.

First and foremost, as always, my wife, Janet, has given me the inspiration to keep doing what I love to do. Even when I'm working around the clock, she never ceases to give me support and words of encouragement. I am truly lucky to have her in my corner. Aside from the moral support, she also helped with the day-to-day editing of my chapters.

My family has always been behind me in everything I do—from dreams of rock 'n' roll stardom, to helping me with school, to my writing. Thanks to my mom and dad, Howard, and Rick. Also, I wouldn't be the responsible person that I am if it weren't for my daughter, Amber. She is a blessing.

Massimo Foti has long been considered one of the top extensionologists in the business. He was our tech editor on the first book, and also on this book. We couldn't have asked for a better person to do the tech editing on an extensions book—the man who won Macromedia's award for Best Extension Writer. In addition to tech editing, Massimo graciously allowed us to use his extensions for some of our examples. For that we are truly grateful. Massimo is the man.

Also, thanks to Jim Schachterle at Osborne for suggesting this book. It has been one of my dreams to write a book about extensions, and Jim had the courage to give us the opportunity. Thanks Jim! Also, thanks to Timothy Madrid and Jennifer Malnick for putting up with us during the creation of this book.

Also, thanks to all the extensionologists out there who have given us support and encouragement. We all learn from each other, and this book is for the people who will come after us. I only wish that we'd had a book like this when we were starting out. Special thanks to Joe Marini, Paul Boon, Jag S. Sidhu, Drew McLellan, Joseph Lowery, Waldo Smeets, and George Petrov.

Finally, my partner Ray West is always there to deal with all the stuff I don't want to deal with. My focus has always been limited, but Ray can do it all, and he does it well. With all the different technologies that are out there and all the specialists, Ray seems to know about all of it. He's one of the geniuses of this business.

—Tom

Ray's Acknowledgements

This was an exciting book to write, but we are truly indebted to the work of many others. Our work builds on the shoulders of some great programmers like David George, Joe Marini, Andrew Wooldridge, Jaro von Flocken, and our good friend and technical editor Massimo Foti. We appreciate all of their work and hope that this book can help to breed a new generation of extensionologists.

I couldn't do anything without my wife, Susan, and my boy, Caleb. They are the reason I work so hard, even when it means I don't have enough time to be with them.

Thanks to all of our great friends in this community who have given us so much encouragement.

And thanks to Tom, whose expertise has kept us on the cutting edge and made it possible for us to have so many great opportunities. Here's to many more.

—Ray

Introduction

You will find several books on the shelves about Dreamweaver and UltraDev, but none, I'll wager, like this one. It's not a big book. It's not a thick book. Certainly not as thick as that one right next to you, *Dreamweaver UltraDev 4: The Complete Reference*. You should pick up a copy of that one too, while you're at it.

But this is an important book if you want to learn how Dreamweaver and UltraDev really work. This is a book about building extensions. Extensions are the building blocks that make up the functionality of these popular programs. Every object, behavior, and command is technically an extension and you can write them using the same platform that Macromedia engineers use.

The extensibility layer of the Dreamweaver products is ingenious. It exposes the core functionality of the programs to an application programming interface (API) that you can manipulate using HTML and JavaScript. That means that anyone with a good understanding of HTML and JavaScript can teach Dreamweaver to do just about anything with point-and-click ease.

Who Should Buy this Book

Anyone who is interested in extending Dreamweaver or UltraDev will find this book an absolute necessity. We do, however, make a few assumptions about you.

- ▶ You are familiar with the basic operation of Dreamweaver and UltraDev.
- ▶ You are very comfortable with HTML.
- ▶ You are somewhat comfortable with JavaScript. We'll walk you through the stickier parts, but you need to be conversational anyway.

Conventions Used in this Book

The following conventions are used in the writing of this book.

Code references use the following font:

```
var strName = "Bob"
```

Sometimes, code that is supposed to be on one line gets broken up because of the width of the page. In that case, there will be a continuation character indicating that you should enter the code on one line. That character looks like this:

¬

When you are supposed to press keys, they will be represented like this:

CTRL-F10

Every attempt has been made to ensure that the code listings and content in the book are accurate. If you find any mistakes, please drop us a line so that we can correct future editions. Also, the code used in the book is available for download from our Web site, **www.basic-ultradev.com**. The best way to go through the tutorials in the book is to download the actual files used and then follow along with the code listings in the book.

To really understand extensions, however, you will need to write your own. Do the exercises at the end of each chapter. Find something that is missing from Dreamweaver that you would like to add, and see if you can make an extension out of it. Many times you'll find something similar to it, but not exactly what you need. Often you can use these extension files as a good starting point for your own extension.

Writing extensions can be a fun and rewarding experience. We hope that you will want to dive into creating your own extensions after reading this book.

Beginning
Dreamweaver
Extensibility

IN THIS CHAPTER:

Things have different meanings to different people. While most are happy to be able to operate their cars safely, some people are not happy unless they can get under the hood and tinker around. Some are content with the latest brand-name computer from the local store shelf, and others have to carefully select and assemble each component by hand and then test the limits of the processor.

Software has become the same way. Programs are shipping with more functionality than ever, yet there is an unmistakable trend toward allowing the end user to get inside and mix things up. The entire suite of Microsoft Office products includes Visual Basic for Applications (VBA), a subset of Visual Basic that allows users to add functionality to Word, Excel, Project, and many other applications. Most users read the manual to find out what a product does. Others read it to find out what it does not do and how they can make it do those things.

Macromedia's product line, including Dreamweaver, UltraDev, Fireworks, and others, is exceptionally capable of performing the tasks for which it was designed. But the creators of these programs were smart enough to realize that users would want more. Well, they were smart enough to realize it when it was shown to them. You see, even though the things that we will discuss in this book are at the very heart of the structure of Macromedia products, they were not always meant for end-user consumption. It took the tireless efforts of some very talented people digging around within the directory structure on their computers to figure out how Dreamweaver worked and to start making it do things that it wasn't originally programmed to do. Their work made Dreamweaver even more popular than it already was and has spawned the community of what are now known as extensionologists: those people for which the base product is not enough.

This book is for people who want to get under the hood of Dreamweaver and UltraDev.

NOTE

We will use the term "Dreamweaver" when referring to the product unless the feature being discussed is specific to UltraDev, such as the data sources and recordsets functionality. Everything that applies to Dreamweaver also apples to UltraDev. The reverse is not necessarily true.

What Is an Extension?

What is meant when we talk about extending Dreamweaver or the extensibility of any product or platform in general? Typically, something is extensible if you can add to it; if you can learn enough about it that you can change its features in some way to make it do things that it wasn't originally able to do. Now, that doesn't mean that when you lose your hammer and have to use the handle of a screwdriver to hang a picture that the screwdriver is extensible. Extensibility is something that is built into a product by providing a methodology that encourages people to find ways to make it grow. A feature or function that you add to a product is called an extension because it extends the core product in some way.

Dreamweaver is extensible because it provides a framework that allows developers with the right skills to add features and functionality that does not exist out of the box. But unlike some products, for which extensibility is almost an afterthought, extensions are the very core of Dreamweaver. In fact, every behavior, every object, every menu item in the base product was created using the exact same platform and methodology that we are going to teach you in this book. There is nothing that Dreamweaver does out of the box that cannot be mimicked or added to in your own extensions because you are using the same tools that the developers at Macromedia used when they originally created the program. This is the fun stuff. It is a truly amazing thing to watch your work become a part of this program in a way that helps you and others become more productive.

An extension in Dreamweaver and UltraDev is essentially a means of inserting code onto a page. It could be HTML, it could be ASP, it could be Cold Fusion or Java or JavaScript. Extensions provide a way to create Web pages without having to hand-code line after line. They are prebuilt ways of generating often-used blocks of the text that makes up these pages based on the input of the user. So, instead of typing an <HR> tag into a text editor, you can drag a Horizontal Rule Object onto your page and see it represented as an actual horizontal rule. And instead of typing in the several lines it takes to create a database connection, define a recordset, open it, and manipulate it, you can select a Server Behavior designed to do this for you based on the properties you set in a graphical user interface. Dreamweaver extensions are the WYS in WYSIWYG.

If you have used Dreamweaver and UltraDev before—and you better have if you hope to understand this book—you have used extensions hundreds of times already even if you never wrote one or downloaded one from a developer or the Macromedia Exchange. Chances are, though, that you have added several features to your copy of Dreamweaver by choosing extensions that provide the functionality you need to do your work. Your copy of Dreamweaver or UltraDev is likely different that any other copy on anyone else's computer.

There are several reasons that people choose to write extensions. Some do it for fun. There is certainly a feeling of accomplishment when you add a feature to such a powerful program that makes it more powerful and fills a need that you have seen in the user community.

Some people do it for the productivity is provides. Especially in a team environment, the development of custom extensions can increase efficiency enormously. And through custom extensions, companies can take advantage of their other development efforts like COM objects and Enterprise Java Beans within Dreamweaver.

There is also a growing community of developers who are creating Dreamweaver extensions as a business. There is certainly a strong market for additional product functionality for those users who bought Dreamweaver and UltraDev so that they would not have to learn to code by hand.

Whatever the reason you are interested in learning to create Dreamweaver extensions, we are glad you are here. You could not have picked a better book.

What Kinds of Extensions Are There?

As mentioned earlier, all the Dreamweaver and UltraDev products are built up with extensions, so everything you see and use is structured as an extension to the core product. Basically, the following types of extensions exist:

- ▶ Behaviors
- ▶ Objects
- ▶ Commands
- ▶ Data Sources
- ▶ Server Behaviors
- ▶ Browser Profiles
- ▶ Floaters
- ▶ Property Inspectors
- ▶ Menus
- ▶ Server Models
- ▶ Third-Party Tags
- ▶ Translators
- ▶ Reports
- ▶ References

Behaviors

Behaviors are used to add client-side (or browser-side) code to your pages in the form of JavaScript functions. They are known as behaviors because they are used to define the ways in which objects on your pages behave in response to user intervention. As such, behaviors are made up of three things: an object, an event, and an action.

The object in this case is the item on your page that you expect the user to interact with. It could be a form button or a block of text or an image—anything that the end user is likely to point to or move or click on your page. That occurrence of user interaction is known as an event.

Events are predefined ways that a user can interact with an object on your page. For a form button, it might be onClick, the process of the user clicking the button with the mouse. For a page itself, it could be onLoad, which occurs when the user causes the page to be loaded in the browser. These events are inherent to the objects themselves and are not the part that you will be creating when you build a behavior.

The part that you will be responsible for when you build a behavior is the action. An action is the thing that happens when a selected event occurs. For instance, you could apply a behavior that calls for an alert box to appear when the user clicks a button (we will build just such a behavior in Chapter 2). In this case, the button is the object, the click is the event, and the alert box is the action.

The typical action is a combination of attributes assigned to objects and JavaScript functions that define the action that is to take place. You will learn to build behaviors in Chapter 2.

Objects

Objects are the most basic form of extension in Dreamweaver. Their purpose is to facilitate the insertion of HTML tags into the pages that you are designing. At its simplest, this can involve an empty tag like the <HR> tag. <HR> inserts a Horizontal Rule and requires no additional properties and no closing tag.

But objects can do much more powerful things than this. They can be made responsible for not only the basic tag insertion, but also for any number of properties that may be associated with a particular tag, such as colors and borders; for sub-tags, such as the number of table row (<tr>) and table data (<td>) tags that appear within the table; and for the selection of included files, like image and rollover image objects.

Objects are one of the easiest extensions to build, and they will be covered in Chapter 2.

Commands

Commands are really the developer's extension. Rather than adding pieces that make up what will become your HTML pages, commands are used to traverse and alter your code to perform frequently needed functions. Commands can find, add, delete, or change almost any part of the code on any page that exists on your local drive, whether it's open or not. They can even create new pages as a part of some larger operation.

A good example of a useful command is the Clean Up Word HTML command that comes with Dreamweaver. When you use Microsoft Word to convert a document to HTML, the resulting page is full of proprietary XML tags and what can best be considered sloppy HTML. The Clean Up Word HTML command has been trained to seek out these extraneous tags and remove them, leaving behind a more standards-compliant, efficient version of the document, a job that would take hours to do by hand for even a moderate sized site.

Commands are often called as parts of other extensions. The recordset Server Behaviors in UltraDev call commands to create the various pieces that are inserted in your pages.

Commands can also be created "macro style" by selecting a number of steps from Dreamweaver's History palette and saving them as commands. This is a good introduction to the power of commands, but you can do much more if you learn how they really work; you will do this in Chapter 3.

Data Sources

Data Sources are just what they sound like. They are the places from which your pages can get the data that they display in UltraDev. The sources that come with UltraDev can be found in the Plus (+) menu of the Data Bindings palette. They include recordsets, commands (as in database Stored Procedures, not the commands discussed previously) and server model–specific items like sessions, requests, and application variables.

Perhaps the most popular of the Data Source extensions is the UltraDev Shopping Cart from PowerClimb Software. The basic component of the "UltraCart" is a data source that communicates with a series of session variables that make up the shopping cart.

Server Behaviors

What behaviors are to the client side of the Web experience, Server Behaviors are to the server side. The functions and procedures that are inserted by Server Behaviors are evaluated at the server and sent to the user as HTML and client-side script. Anything that needs to be done at the server in any of UltraDev's supported server models (and even others if you would like to attempt to create a server model) can be encapsulated in a Server Behavior.

Like other extensions, Server Behaviors range from simple one-line code insertions to complex combinations of head and body code. They can be self-contained or rely on considerable interaction from the end user to supply parameters for the code that will be inserted. They can call commands to perform more complicated code editing tasks.

Writing Server Behaviors from scratch is a complicated job requiring a good knowledge of JavaScript, but that is the only way that many of them can be built. For more straightforward Server Behaviors, UltraDev 4 comes with the Server Behavior Builder that automates many of the parts of the task. Both methods are covered in Chapter 5.

Browser Profiles

One of the most important issues that continues to plague Web developers is cross-browser compatibility. The ability to write code that displays correctly in browsers that keep changing is the Holy Grail of designers everywhere. This issue is complicated when you are trusting a product like Dreamweaver to insert code for you, especially DHTML-type code.

Dreamweaver tries to help you out by identifying which of its extensions are usable for the variety of browsers that are available. To do this, it uses Browser Profiles that delineate the abilities of each browser brand and version. As new browsers are released, or if you are concerned about a browser that is not included in the base product, you can add browser profiles that follow the feature set that is important to you.

Floaters

You can't miss floaters. They assault you from the moment you open Dreamweaver, hanging as if unsupported all around the screen and often getting in the way of the page you are trying to design. But they are also useful. Floaters (often called palettes) are the containers that house all of the tools that you will use to build pages in Dreamweaver.

Within a new floater, you can house any number of new functionalities. For instance, one of the authors constructed a floater that houses a JavaScript evaluator that is useful for debugging code in your pages.

Building floaters is covered in Chapter 4.

Inspectors

Property Inspectors are a special kind of floater that allow you to view the properties of the tag that is currently selected. For instance, if you have an image highlight, the Property Inspector will automatically display things like the image's name, the path to its file, and where you will go if you click it.

Property Inspectors are an important part of several kinds of extensions, and you will need to create them in order to have complete implementations of Objects, Server Behaviors, and other extensions. They not only allow you to view properties, but also to edit them outside the actual extension interface.

Building Property Inspectors is covered in Chapter 4.

Menus

Like any modern program, Dreamweaver is built around a set of menus that provide access (sometimes redundant access) to its functionality. The menu structure of Dreamweaver is contained within an XML file that is extensible to include your own code. You may insert items into menus through your extensions, or you may find other reasons to add menu items. Menus are covered in Chapter 6.

Server Models

UltraDev comes with support for three server platforms: ASP, JSP, and CFML. A Server Model is all of the many extensions that are required to define the basic functionality of UltraDev in a particular platform including recordsets, Repeat Regions, session control, and form behavior. A PHP server model has recently been released by a third party, so the four most popular platforms are available, but others do exist including Cache Server Pages and a variety of proprietary platforms that could be implemented as Server Models.

Third-Party Tags

Using Third-Party Tags, you can define to Dreamweaver the properties that make up a tag set so that they can be used and represented in the program. For example, you might define a car tag that has properties like number of doors or color. The information in these tags can then be integrated into an XML data scheme that makes it easy to represent your specialized data in your Web pages.

We will examine Third-Party Tags in the Objects discussion in Chapter 2.

Translators

Translators are very important to the WYSIWYG concept in Dreamweaver. Without translators, the code that is created could only be represented by a generic placeholder that tells you that there is code present but does not tell you anything about it in the Design view of your pages. A good example is the way UltraDev handles the insertion of recordset fields into your pages. If you drag a field called ID from a recordset call Login onto your page you will see {Login.ID} at that spot on your page, indicating that it contains the code that displays the information from the ID field of the recordset. Without a translator that converts the code into this representation, you would only see an ASP shield that tells you that there is ASP code present, but not what it does.

Reports

Using Dreamweaver's reporting function, you can run reports about various aspects of your site. HTML reports tell you things like which documents in your site are currently untitled or have nested font tags that need to be cleaned up. Workflow reports can tell you who has pages checked out, and File Reports can list the dates that files were created and their current sizes. You can create reports to display other kinds of information about your site.

References

New to version 4, Dreamweaver's references provide immediate, context sensitive access to information about various topics like ASP syntax, HTML, and other languages. You can create online references to provide information about other programming topics, extensions, or anything else that users might find useful to access within Dreamweaver.

Building Extensions

Dreamweaver and UltraDev extensions are built using HTML and JavaScript. This makes for quite an interesting scenario, in that you can use Dreamweaver to extend itself. The files that are created are nothing more than HTML that defines a user interface and JavaScript that contains the functions that are called to make the extension do its work. If you are good at HTML and JavaScript, you have a head start toward writing your own extensions.

NOTE

Dreamweaver extensions make use of the entirety of the JavaScript programming language, meaning that if all you have done in JavaScript is browser manipulation, you may need a good reference to get you up to speed on the more advanced capabilities of the language.

Another important part of the puzzle is the use of Regular Expressions (RegExps) to identify and alter code patterns. Regular Expressions are an outgrowth of the Perl language and are available in both JavaScript and VBScript. They are amazingly powerful, and their use is key to the power of Dreamweaver's extensibility layer. They can look intimidating at first, but once you get used to the syntax, you will find a myriad of uses for them.

However, JavaScript will not allow you to do everything you might want to. Limitations of the language make it incapable of doing things like reading and writing to files on your hard drive. Also, being a scripting language, it is interpreted and its source code is available to be viewed and altered by the end user. To accommodate more advanced needs, there is a C extensibility layer available that allows you to encapsulate code within dynamic link libraries. You can use these to perform functions that JavaScript cannot or to hide your code where it is safe from prying and stealing eyes.

NOTE

Traditionally, extensions are a somewhat open source type of item. Many extension builders have gotten their start by examining and borrowing the code of the extension greats like Massimo Foti, Andrew Wooldridge, and Jaro von Flocken. Increasingly, though, more advanced extensions are being created within business models that are funded through the sale of the extensions. In these cases, it is obviously advantageous to be able to keep the methods your extension employs secret from competing developers. Good people have different opinions on the direction the extensions community should go in this regard, but the ability is there to use if you so choose.

The Configurations Folder

The extensions that make up Dreamweaver exist within the Configuration folder and its subfolders. It is from the contents of these folders that Dreamweaver configures itself and loads the available extensions at startup, so your extensions will go here alongside those that ship with the product.

Beneath the root Dreamweaver folder, you will find the Configuration folder, and beneath that, a series of folders corresponding to the different types of extensions that are available in the product. The files in these folders correspond directly to the different areas of Dreamweaver that are extensible. For example, every item on the Commands menu of Dreamweaver has a corresponding HTML file in the Configuration | Commands folder. Every object in the Objects floater has corresponding files in the Configuration | Objects folder. By modifying these or creating your own, you can effectively change the functionality of Dreamweaver. Within these folders you will find two types of files that make up the extensions:

▶   HTML User Interface

▶   JavaScript and XML Code Files

The User Interface

Most extensions have an *interface* for receiving attributes from the user. This interface can be designed inside of the Dreamweaver environment because it is an HTML form. There are several ways to go about designing it. Generally, it is recommended to start with a basic table and add your attributes to it, as shown in Figure 1-1.

When you are designing your interface, remember that you will be referring to the items extensively in your code. It is certainly easier to keep track of the elements of your interface if your text field is named firstRowColor rather than textfield2.

While you are certainly free to do as you like, there are additional considerations if you intend to submit your extension for Macromedia approval and want it to resemble what users are used to seeing. You might think that your extension looks great in purple, but Macromedia has strict guidelines that you should follow to remain 100 percent compatible:

▶   Don't use font or background colors. These will be standard Dreamweaver/UltraDev colors that are picked by default.

▶   Don't use font styles.

► Your company or personal logo can be in the interface, but it should be on the bottom. Alternatively, you can put an About button on the interface and link to an HTML page or another tab in your interface.

► You can include a brief help text in the interface itself with a color set to #D3D3D3.

► Extensions should have a Help button.

These are just a few of the guidelines. A full list can be found in the file ui_guidelines.html under C:\Program Files\Macromedia\Extension Manager\Help (if you installed to the default directory on Windows).

TIP

To remove all styles, colors, and fonts from the page, design your interface in the Dreamweaver environment and then edit it in Homesite, BBEdit, or your text editor of choice.

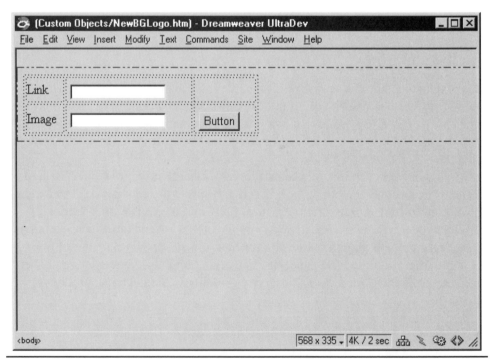

Figure 1-1   *Typical basic extension interface design*

JavaScript Code

If you follow the latest construction scheme for Dreamweaver extensions, you will house your JavaScript in a separate file from your user interface. In addition to the HTML elements, your interface should have a line at the top to import the JavaScript functions that are used in the execution of the extension, such as:

```
<script src="myextension.js"></script>
```

This file should have the same name as your HTML file except with a .js extension. When you have your interface file ready, it can be saved into the appropriate folder under Configuration.

Most of the hard work of writing extensions is hand-coding JavaScript into the .js file for manipulating the document, which can be done more efficiently in Homesite, BBEdit, or your editor of choice. The JavaScript code that is contained in this file has a few basic functions:

▶ Gets the attributes from the form that was submitted (the interface).

▶ Gets pertinent information from the document being edited, such as the current selection, or the insertion point.

▶ Puts the user-defined attributes into a string with the HTML and script that is to be inserted into the document.

▶ Inserts the resulting string into the user's document.

The particulars of how these extension elements relate to the various extension types will be covered as we get into each type.

The Document Object Model

The Dreamweaver extensibility layer is based on a combination of the W3C Document Object Model and the Netscape Document Object Model. This does not mean that extensions have any special affinity for Netscape, only that the sets of functions that are used to interact with your pages and their accompanying notation are based on the model that is used in the Netscape browser. The real power of Dreamweaver's extensions is the over 300 additional functions in the Application Programming Interface (API) that are particular to the Dreamweaver product. They combine to make it possible to manipulate your pages in an endless variety of ways.

There are several things you need to understand about how Dreamweaver goes about searching and building code in your pages. The particulars will be covered as we work through examples in the following chapters. For now you should be aware of:

▶ Selections and offsets

▶ Nodes

▶ Dot notation

Selections and Offsets

Sometimes extension writing is a fairly simple procedure, but other times it may require some very complex document and string manipulation, as in the case of Server Behaviors. The same principles apply to all extensions, though, from the basic Objects to the complex Server Behaviors. Depending on what your extension is doing, it is going to work with a *selection*, which is a highlighted area on the page, or an *insertion point,* where your cursor is currently located. Here is an example of using the getSelection() method of Dreamweaver, which is a function from the Dreamweaver API for getting a selection:

```
var theSelection = dreamweaver.getSelection();
```

This function will return an array of two values that represent the beginning of the selection and the end of the selection as *offsets* to the beginning of the document. To see whether there is an actual selection made, or if you are just talking about an insertion point, check to see whether the two values match, meaning there is nothing selected. You can do that with a block like this:

```
if (theSelection[0] == theSelection[1]) {
//we have an nsertion point, not a selection
}else{
//we have  selection
};
```

This function can be used both ways, and it can be used to display an error message if the extension requires a selection and the user hasn't selected anything.

You can then manipulate the document yourself using the powerful function dw.getDocumentDom(), which will return the contents of the document in object form. You do that like this:

```
var theDom = dw.getDocumentDom('document');
```

The object that is returned, theDom, can be used to get the actual selection in text format by first getting the documentElement property of the document node (theDom). Once you have that, you use the outerHTML property of the documentElement to get the actual text of the entire document:

```
var theDom = dw.getDocumentDom('document');
var theSelection = dreamweaver.getSelection();
var theEntireDocument = theDom.documentElement.outerHTML;
var theSelectedText = theEntireDocument.substring(theSelection[0],
theSelection[1]);
```

Now, the variable theSelectedText contains the actual text that is highlighted in the document window. If this happens to be an object like an image, the variable will contain the entire object, including tags and attributes. You can start to see now that this becomes very powerful indeed for both inserting things into your document and editing things that are already in your document. Highlighting an image, for example, will put the contents of the entire HTML code block for rendering that image into the variable, which can then be manipulated, altered, or given behaviors.

TIP

Another way to highlight a block of HTML on the page is to click the tag name in the lower-left corner of the document window.

You can also get the text before the selection or the text after the selection using the selection and the offsets to the selection. Added to the previous example, the following lines of code will return the two blocks of text around the selection:

```
var beforeTheSelectedText = theEntireDocument.substring(0,
theSelection[0]);
var afterTheSelectedText =
theEntireDocument.substring(theSelection[1]);
```

The first example (before selection) starts at the zero position on the page and gets all text up to the beginning of the selection. The second line gets all text starting at the point where the selection ends. This gives you three parts: before the selection, the selection, and after the selection. You can easily take these three parts of the page and put them back together or manipulate the text in one or more of the parts. Let's say you wanted to make the selection a link. You could do that with a simple <a href> tag around the selection, like this:

```
theSelection = ' <a href="http://www.myhomepage.com">' +
theSelectedText + '</a>';
```

Notice that you just concatenated the string with the opening tag, the selection, and the closing tag. Now theSelection variable holds the original selection wrapped in a link. To write it back to the page, you have to concatenate the strings together like this:

```
var theDom = dw.getDocumentDom('document');
theDom.outerHTML = beforeTheSelectedText + theSelection + afterTheSelectedText;
```

Now your updated page contains a link around the text that you selected.

Nodes

Previously, we mentioned the document *node*. Nodes are essential to the understanding of the DOM, both in browsers and in Dreamweaver extensions and are required for some of the complex HTML manipulation within Dreamweaver. Every tag in the document is a node. Nodes have many properties that can be used by the developer to build extensions. The properties are accessed through standard *dot* notation, as in myNode.property (pronounced "my node dot property"). There are four basic types of nodes, which can be checked with the nodeType property:

▶ **DOCUMENT_NODE** The document level node; allows you to have access to all parts of the document.

▶ **ELEMENT_NODE** A node for an HTML tag, such as `<table>`.

▶ **COMMENT_NODE** An HTML comment surrounded by `<!-- -->`.

▶ **TEXT_NODE** A block of text that is on the page.

To better understand nodes, examine the following:

```
<table>
    <tr>
     <td>First</td>
     <td>Last</td>
     <!--this is a comment node-->
    </tr>
</table>
```

The `<table>` tag is the outermost node in the example. It is an ELEMENT type node and contains nodes within, called *child nodes,* which are accessible through the

childNodes property of the table node. The one item in the childNodes array is the
<tr> node. That node has a childNodes array as well, with three items in it: two
<td> tag pairs and a COMMENT type node. Nodes also have parents, accessible
through the parentNode property. The parentNode of <tr> is the <table> node.
Not seen here is the parent of the <table>, the <body> node. Parent to the <body>
node is the <html> node, which is the DOCUMENT nodeType.

You've already seen the outerHTML property of the document node; this was the
entire document, including the tags that made up the node. Another property is the
innerHTML property, which, as you might guess, gets what is between the tags. This
property is useful for getting text that is contained within a tag. Another handy property
of a node is the tagName property. The tagName property of the <table> tag is
"table," which you could use in a situation where you are looking for a particular
node, like this:

```
for (i=0; i<someNodes.length; i++) {
  if(someNodes[i].tagName == "table") {
  //found a table tag--do some stuff to it
  };
};
```

You can use this method to your advantage if you are trying to insert some code
into a specific tag, such as adding a JavaScript rollover behavior to an image tag
or putting some server-side code into a repeat-region table tag to alternate colored
rows. Or, you could write your own custom tag, such as <TM:MYTAG>, put it
into the Custom Tags folder (which we'll get to later) and then check whether
myNode.tagName is equal to "TM:MYTAG". Another way to find a tag is to use
the function findTag(tagName), located in the DOM.js file.

TIP

*This is a quick and dirty way to recognize your own code in a page, especially during the
debugging phase of your extension writing.*

Dot Notation

Accessing properties of the DOM or objects in the DOM is done with standard
dot notation, and it's time to take a closer look at how this works in Dreamweaver.
The root of the tree is the document, and all objects can be accessed through it. The
objects that you will be accessing will be predominantly form items, such as text
fields (or edit boxes), check boxes, radio buttons, and drop-down select boxes.

Getting to these is easy through the document root. Start with document.formname to get the form and then access your form element through its name, like this:

```
document.formname.elementname
```

Depending on what kind of element it is, different properties will be associated with it. A check box will have a "checked" property; a text field will have a "text" property. The code looks like this:

```
var isCheckboxChecked = document.myForm.myCheckbox.checked;
var myText = document.myForm.myTextfield.text;
```

Dot notation can be pretty complicated, but once you are able to follow the logic of it, it is easy to get the properties of any object. The following is a little more complex. Say that you have a select box in an HTML form that will access a list of recordsets available to the page. Once the user has made a selection, you will be able to retrieve it. Start with a select box on the form named selectRecordset. You can use dot notation like this to retrieve the text:

```
var myRecordset =
document.forms[0].selectRecordset.options[document.forms[0].
selectRecordset.selectedIndex].text;
```

Start with "document" and get to the "forms" array next. As you have only one form on the page, access the first element in the array, which has a zero index: forms[0] . If you knew the name of the form, you could use that in its place, but forms[0] is a good general purpose way of getting the form object on a page. Next, access the name of the element in the form selectRecordset. The options of the select box are numbered from 0 to however many recordsets are on the page, so pick the option that is selected. There's no selectedOption property, but there is a selectedIndex property. Since you need the actual text and not the index, access the DOM again with document.forms[0].selectRecordset.selectedIndex to get your [index] number. Now you have the selected option value from the box and all that remains is to get the text of that option. Do that with the text property.

You could organize this into more easily readable lines like this:

```
var theForm = document.forms[0];
var theSelectBox = theForm.selectRecordset;
var theIndex = theSelectBox.selectedIndex;
var theOption = theSelectBox.options[theIndex];
var theText = theOption.text;
```

However, this approach may be a little extreme. In any event, you can see how the hierarchical approach is implemented in the DOM.

JavaScript API Methods

The DOM also has methods. Methods could be considered built-in functions. To access the methods of the DOM, you use dot-notation as well:

```
theNode.theMethod(); //pronounced "the node dot the method"
```

This is a brief list of some of the popular methods. For a full list, consult the Extending Dreamweaver document in the built-in Dreamweaver help system, under the JavaScript API heading.

getElementsByTagName(tagName)

You call this method with a node or with the entire DOM. If you were searching for all images on the page, you would call it like this:

```
var myImageNodeList =
dreamweaver.getDocumentDOM().getElementsByTagName("img");
```

or

```
var theDom = dreamweaver.getDocumentDOM();
var myImageNodeList = theDom.getElementsByTagName("img");
```

hasChildNodes()

This method returns true or false. Use it to determine whether there are child nodes within the node that you are calling it from, as in:

```
if (myNode.hasChildNodes()) {
 //do this
};
```

getAttribute(attrName)

Use this method if you need to find any given attribute of a node. If your node (myNode) contained the following text, you could get the image source path with myNode.getAttribute("src"):

```
<img src="myImage" height=30 width=40>
```

setAttribute(attrName, attrValue)

This method does the opposite of getAttribute and returns no value. You supply the attribute name and the value you want the attribute to have, and setAttribute will write the HTML to your page for you. For example, if you have a table node named myTable and you want to set the width to 50 percent with a click, put the following line in a command:

```
myTable.setAttribute("width","50%");
```

removeAttribute(attrName)

This method removes a given attribute as well as its value from a node.

   As mentioned earlier, Dreamweaver has over 300 built-in functions that can be used to your benefit. This is just the tip of the iceberg. We'll be going through more of these as we build extensions throughout this book.

deleteSelection()

This method of the DOM deletes the current selection of code or text in the currently active document. You can call it like this:

```
var theDom = dw.getDocumentDOM();
theDom.deleteSelection();
```

insertHTML(contentToInsert, bReplaceCurrentSelection)

This is a simple method of the DOM used to insert some HTML code at the current insertion point. The second parameter, bReplaceCurrentSelection, is optional. It is a Boolean value that you can set to true if you want the HTML code to replace the current selection. If you set this to false, the HTML content will be inserted after the selection. You can call the function like this:

```
var theDom = dw.getDocumentDOM();
theDom.insertHTML("<b>My Code</b>",false);
```

insertObject()

Another method of the DOM, this one allows you to insert an Object from the Objects folder into the document at the insertion point. Object names are unique, even between folders, so you can call the Object by name with this method and the Object will be inserted. It is called like this (inserting a form button):

```
var theDom = dw.getDocumentDOM();
theDom.insertObject("Button");
```

insertText()

This method of the DOM allows you to insert text. If you use HTML code using this method, the code will be converted to the text equivalent. For example, inserting the text <table> will cause the text <table> to be inserted:

```
var theDom = dw.getDocumentDOM();
theDom.insertText("<table>");
```

This will show in the document window as <table> as well.

Shared Folder Functions

You don't want to reinvent the wheel when writing your extensions, so it's always a good idea to reuse whatever you can. In addition to the standard methods of the DOM, there are literally hundreds of functions in the Shared folder under Configuration— some are well documented and some aren't. Once you learn your way around the shared folder, you'll be writing extensions much more quickly. Certain repetitive tasks are streamlined by using the appropriate function. Many of the shared folder functions are described in Appendix A.

Display Help

Building a help file is something you might want to consider if your extension is complex or requires any special instructions. The help file can be a basic HTML page with instructions or a complex series of pages with images and hyperlinks. However you decide to do it, the basic method for displaying a help file is with the displayHelp() function. This is a function that Dreamweaver will look for when a user accesses your extension. If the function exists in your extension file in any form, the extension interface will have a Help button below the Cancel and OK buttons. Certain extensions, such as the Floater and the Property Inspector, will have a little question mark (?) on the interface that acts as the help button. By clicking the question mark icon, the displayHelp() function is called.

At its most basic level, the displayHelp() function can just flash an alert box like this:

```
function displayHelp() {
 var alertText = "Choose two styles from the drop down lists\n"
```

```
alertText += "or click the 'New' button to create new styles."
alert(alertText);
 }
```

At a more advanced level, you can use the built-in `browseDocument(path)` function of Dreamweaver. This function will cause your default browser to pop up with the Web page that is passed to the function. You can call the function like this:

```
dreamweaver.browseDocument(myHelpPage);
```

or

```
dw.browseDocument(myHelpPage);
```

NOTE

Keep in mind that you have to pass the entire path to the function or Dreamweaver won't know where to find it.

There is another built-in function that allows you to find the path of the Dreamweaver program on the hard drive that works on both the Mac and in Windows. The function is called `getConfigurationPath()` and will return the full path to the Configuration folder. It's called like this:

```
var pathToConfig = dw.getConfigurationPath();
```

Once you have that information, you can append the location of your help file to it, like this:

```
var helpDoc = "/Shared/MyFolder/Helpdocs/myExtensionHelp.htm";
var fullPath = pathToConfig + helpDoc;
```

The full display help function for the CustomTable object would look like this:

```
function displayHelp() {
 var pathToConfig = dw.getConfigurationPath();
 var helpDoc = "/Shared/MyFolder/Helpdocs/myExtensionHelp.htm";
 var fullPath = pathToConfig + helpDoc;
}
```

Instead of putting a help file into the shared folder, you could have it on the Web somewhere and just point to your Web site, using the full path of the file, like this:

```
dw.browseDocument("http://www.mysite.com/help/myExtensionHelp.htm");
```

What to Take Away from this Chapter

Extending Dreamweaver can seem like an overwhelming task, but it is manageable if you break it down into its parts. As with anything, there are things that each of the extension types have in common and there are techniques that, once you learn them, will become second nature to you. With this book, a good JavaScript reference, and the Macromedia Extending Dreamweaver documentation you have all you need to become highly proficient at this new art of extensibility.

Extending Dreamweaver Documents

This book can teach you how to extend Dreamweaver, but it is not intended as a replacement for the extensibility documentation that comes with Dreamweaver and UltraDev. These documents, which identify and define all of the functions that make up the extensibility layer, are a must for reference and study. They come in electronic form with the program, or you can order a printed copy from Macromedia.

Once you have a handle on these basics, we can dive right into examples of how to build specific Dreamweaver and UltraDev extensions. You can refer back to the information in this chapter, to a good JavaScript Reference, and to the Dreamweaver extensibility documents as you go. Between these three sources, you should have all you need to become an expert extensions builder.

In the next chapter, we will begin with Dreamweaver Behaviors and Objects.

Objects and Behaviors

IN THIS CHAPTER:

W e will begin with what are the most straightforward, if not the easiest, extensions to build. Objects and Behaviors form the core of Dreamweaver's functionality. They mimic the two most basic functions that Web designers perform: the insertion of HTML and client-side JavaScript onto a page.

Objects

Dreamweaver comes with a set of objects that give drag-and-drop capability to the basic set of HTML constructs including tables, layers, images, framesets, and others. They can be found on the Objects palette shown in Figure 2-1.

Figure 2-1   *The Dreamweaver Objects palette*

You will notice that the default palette lists object that are designated as Common. A drop-down box also allows you to view and select objects in other categories such as Form, Hidden, and Frames. We will look at how this is accomplished and how you can add your own categories a little later in this chapter.

Objects, like most extensions, are made up of a combination of HTML and JavaScript, either in one or a series of files. The more contemporary method of creating objects is to put the user interface in an HTML file and the accompanying JavaScript in a file of the same name with a .js file extension.

Objects are designed to place HTML in your page at the insertion point you choose. As specified, they include a standard function called `objectTag()` that returns a string of HTML text. They can be as simple as the Horizontal Rule object shown here:

```
<html>
<head>
<!-- Copyright 1999 Macromedia, Inc. All rights reserved. -->
<title>Insert Horizontal Rule</title>
<script language="javascript">
//--------------    API FUNCTIONS    --------------
function objectTag() {
  // Return the html tag that should be inserted
  return "<HR>";
}
</script>
</head>
<body>
</body>
</html>
```

or they can be as complex as you can imagine; for example, accepting user input from a dialog box and performing calculations to arrive at the return value.

When an object is called, Dreamweaver looks for this `objectTag()` function. If it finds it, it returns the calculated return value to your insertion point. If it doesn't find the function, UltraDev inserts any HTML within the body tags of the objects code into your page. And, if there is no body tag, any HTML code in the file is returned. This makes it a virtual no-brainer to create an object that returns something to your page. Whether that something is valuable or even usable is up to you.

To begin, consider a simple object that places a company logo on the page along with its associated link to the company's home page. It is common for a company to want its logo on each page of its site in order to imprint the brand name on the user and to provide a convenient navigation link back to the home page. The company could insert the logo as an image each time and set the HREF link manually, but most sites end up with a large number of pages, and it would be easier to have an object that could be dragged and dropped from the Objects palette whenever it was needed.

The first step is to come up with some code that works independently of the object itself. This is a simple object that does no calculation. It simply returns a string of HTML to the point where your cursor is placed. You can generate that string as if you were inserting it into the page manually and then cut and paste it into the objectTag() function of your object. If you were going to insert an image called ourlogo.gif from the Images directory of your site into your page and link it to your home page, the HTML would look something like the following. Since you will be pasting this line into a JavaScript function that expects a string, use the single quote (') rather than the double quote (") you'd use if you were going to hand-code.

```
<a href='www.ourhomepage.com'><img src='images/ourlogo.gif' width='182'
height='44' border='0'></a>
```

You could cut and paste this line into a layer or the cell of a table and it would always do the same thing: place the company logo on the page with a link to the home page. This makes it ideal code for an object, because no matter where your insertion point falls on the page, this code will make sense—if not from a design standpoint, at least from a functional one.

You can even use the framework of the HR object you looked at earlier to get started. Pasting the HTML in and changing the Macromedia copyright makes it look like this:

```
<html>
<head>
<!-- Copyright 2000 ourhomepage.com All rights reserved. -->
<title>Insert Logo</title>
<script language="javascript">
//--------------      API FUNCTIONS      --------------
function objectTag() {
  // Return the html tag that should be inserted
  return "<a href='www.ourhomepage.com'><img src='images/ourlogo.gif' width='182'
height='44' border='0'></a>";
}
</script>
</head>
<body>
</body>
</html>
```

Since there is an `objectTag()` function in the object, Dreamweaver will use its return value and insert the line of code in your page.

All you really need to do to get this object to work in Dreamweaver is save it and restart the program. It is important, however, where you save it, since Dreamweaver looks for objects in a certain set of folders on your hard drive. You need to get to your configuration folder. On a PC with a default installation, the path is C:\Program Files\Macromedia\Dreamweaver\Configuration. Inside that folder you will see additional folders with names you may recognize like Commands, Behaviors, Menus, and so on, seen in Figure 2-2. Open the Objects folder. Since you are building an object, it is a pretty safe bet that it belongs somewhere in the Objects folder.

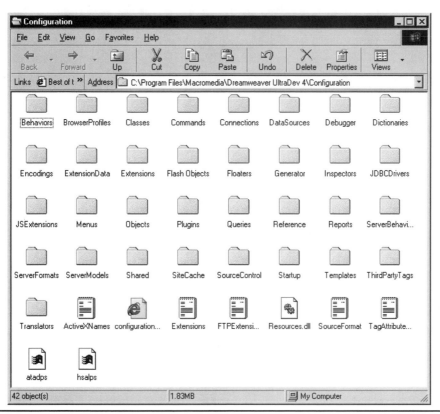

Figure 2-2   *The Configuration folder*

Inside the Objects folder, you will see a number of folders with names like Common, Forms, and Frames. You may notice that these names correspond to the tabs on the Objects palette in Dreamweaver. Could it be so easy that adding another folder beneath the Objects folder adds another tab with your custom name and object on it? Yes, it could… and it is. Create a folder called Custom and open it. Save your object code file to this folder. Name it SiteURL.html. When you close and reopen Dreamweaver, you will see another tab on the Objects palette called Custom with your `SiteURL()` object ready to be dropped on the page, as in Figure 2-3.

TIP

Alternatively, you can hold down the CTRL key and click the arrow in the Objects palette that is used to select the Object category. You will see a Reload Extension menu item at the bottom of the pop-up box. Click it to reload your objects, including your new one, without leaving Dreamweaver.

Figure 2-3   *The Objects palette with your Custom category*

While this works well, you may be asking why your Object is represented with a little question mark instead of a cool logo like all of the others. Well, as smart as Dreamweaver is, it doesn't really know what your object does or how it should be represented. But you can tell it.

If you snoop around in some of the folders underneath the Objects folder, you will notice that for every HTML object file, there is also a GIF file with the same name. It is this GIF file that Dreamweaver uses to visually represent your object on the Objects palette. All you need is an 18×18 pixel GIF file saved in your Custom objects folder with the same name as your HTML file and a GIF extension (SiteURL.gif). Reloading your Objects palette again will display your Object with its own custom icon. Now placing that logo on each and every page within your site will not be quite the pain that it would have been without this newfound knowledge.

A More Complex Object

Simple objects can be created to save time and effort when you need to perform tasks over and over. But objects can also be used to encapsulate things other than HTML constructs. For instance, you may need to place a series of items on your pages that interface with an external system like a content management solution. Or you may have designed an XML specification that utilizes a system of custom tags that need to be read from your pages. These are great candidates for objects. Let's look at an object that makes use of a third-party tag to define data on your pages.

This object uses a form to accept input from the user and takes advantage of Dreamweaver's ability to handle third-party tags. It allows you to place a Car object on your page and set Model, Horsepower, and Cylinders attributes. Within standard HTML, it is not terribly useful, but if you ever needed to pass around automobile information in XML, this would be a great addition to your Objects palette.

While you could choose any number or combination of attributes for your object, this object uses three: Model, Horsepower, and Cylinders. The Model is selected from a drop-down box on a user interface. The Horsepower field is a text box that will accept any number up to three digits, and the Cylinders property is a set of radio buttons with four choices: 4, 6, 8, and 12. The first thing you'll need to do is design and code your user interface, as shown in Figure 2-4. Thankfully, that is something that Dreamweaver is very good at.

In Dreamweaver, create a new HTML page. You will be submitting a form to Dreamweaver to pass in the user's input, so go ahead and place a Form object on the page. You will need three sets of inputs, each with an identifying label. In order to get this to line up nicely, go ahead and put a 3×3 table on the page and put three

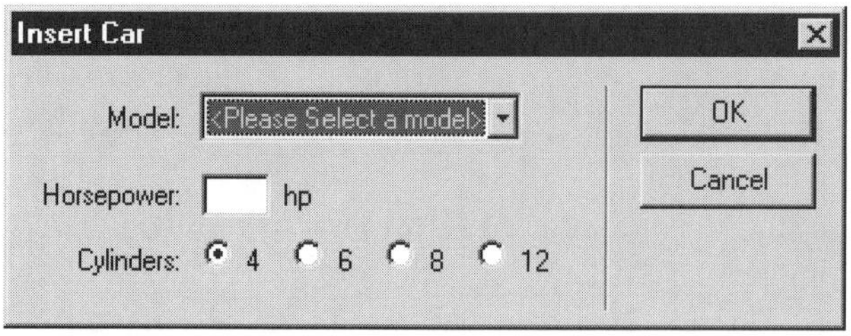

Figure 2-4   *The Car object user interface*

labels in the left-hand column cells: Models:, Horsepower:, and Cylinders: (see Figure 2-5).

In the top right cell, place a drop-down box. Name it Model and make it a menu type. Your list of values can be as long or short as you would like. The list in the included code contains a number of automobile brands. Feel free to add any more that you can think of. The top choice should be some sort of Please Select entry to prompt the user to select a model. The list should contain your model names as the Item Label and as the Value, as shown in Figure 2-6.

In the second cell of the right hand column, next to the Horsepower label, place a single-line text box. Name it Horsepower and set its character width to 6 or so and its max length to 3.

In the third cell of the right-hand column, place four radio buttons. They should be labeled 4, 6, 8, and 12 with corresponding checked values. Name all four of the radio buttons Cylinders. Naming them the same name identifies these buttons as a part of a group and allows you to access them as a collection later.

That's all you need to do for the design of your page. UltraDev will handle the placement of an OK button and a Cancel button, so you don't need to worry about how your form gets submitted. Just leave it with a default method and leave the name and action properties blank. Change the title of the page to Insert Car and go

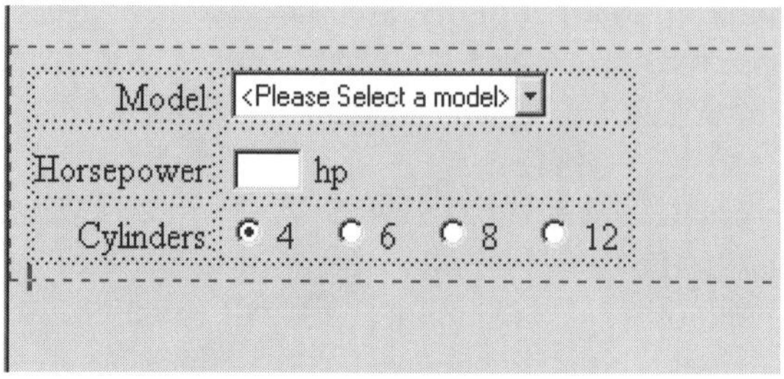

Figure 2-5   *Building the Car object user interface*

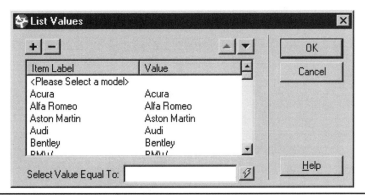

Figure 2-6 *The user interface List Values*

ahead and save this page as car.htm. There is more happening behind the scenes, but you are done with the visual design of your object.

Coding Your Object

You need to hand-code some things into the `objectTag()` function we talked about earlier to accept your user's input and use it in the object. The entire code listing is available, shown next. Following is a breakdown of each step with an explanation of what is happening.

```
<html>
<head>
<title>Insert Car</title>
<script language="JavaScript">
function objectTag() {
  /* save the form object in a variable for convenience */
  var theForm = document.forms[0];
/*
 model is an exclusive select list (only one option can be selected at a time).
get the selectedIndex property of the field and read the value of the option at
that position to determine which model is selected.
*/
  var model = theForm.model.options[theForm.model.selectedIndex].value;
  /*
horsepower is a text field. its value can be read directly.
  */
  var horsepower = theForm.horsepower.value;
```

```
  /*
determine which of the cylinders options is selected.
  */
  var cylinders;
  for (var i=0; i < theForm.cylinders.length; i++) {
          if (theForm.cylinders[i].checked) {
                  cylinders = theForm.cylinders[i].value;
                  break;
                  }
                  }
  /*
initialize attributes as an empty string. this is where the attributes and their
values will be stored.
  */
  var attributes = "";
  /* add the individual attributes to the attributes string. */
  attributes += ' model="' + model + '"';
  attributes += ' horsepower="' + horsepower + '"';
  attributes += ' cylinders="' + cylinders + '"';
  /* return the CAR tag */
  return "<CAR" + attributes + ">";
}
</script>
</head>
<body>
<form>
<table border="0">
<tr>
<td align="right" valign="baseline">Model:</td>
<td valign="baseline" colspan="3">
<select name="model">
<option value="" selected>&lt;Please Select a model&gt;</option>
<option value="Acura">Acura</option>
<option value="Alfa Romeo">Alfa Romeo</option>
<option value="Aston Martin">Aston Martin</option>
<option value="Audi">Audi</option>
<option value="Bentley">Bentley</option>
<option value="BMW">BMW</option>
<option value="Buick">Buick</option>
<option value="Cadillac">Cadillac</option>
<option value="Chevrolet">Chevrolet</option>
<option value="Chrysler">Chrysler</option>
<option value="Daewoo">Daewoo</option>
<option value="Daihatsu">Daihatsu</option>
<option value="Dodge">Dodge</option>
```

```
<option value="Eagle">Eagle</option>
<option value="Ferrari">Ferrari</option>
<option value="Fiat">Fiat</option>
<option value="Ford">Ford</option>
<option value="Geo">Geo</option>
<option value="GMC">GMC</option>
<option value="Honda">Honda</option>
<option value="Hyundai">Hyundai</option>
<option value="Infiniti">Infiniti</option>
<option value="Isuzu">Isuzu</option>
<option value="Jaguar">Jaguar</option>
<option value="Jeep">Jeep</option>
<option value="Kia">Kia</option>
<option value="Lamborghini">Lamborghini</option>
<option value="Land Rover">Land Rover</option>
<option value="Lexus">Lexus</option>
<option value="Lincoln">Lincoln</option>
<option value="Lotus">Lotus</option>
<option value="Mazda">Mazda</option>
<option value="Mercedes Benz">Mercedes Benz</option>
<option value="Mercury">Mercury</option>
<option value="Merkur">Merkur</option>
<option value="MG">MG</option>
<option value="Misubishi">Mitsubishi</option>
<option value="Nissan">Nissan</option>
<option value="Oldsmobile">Oldsmobile</option>
<option value="Plymouth">Plymouth</option>
<option value="Pontiac">Pontiac</option>
<option value="Porche">Porche</option>
<option value="Peugeot">Peugeot</option>
<option value="Renault">Renault</option>
<option value="Rolls Royce">Rolls Royce</option>
<option value="Saab">Saab</option>
<option value="Saturn">Saturn</option>
<option value="Sterling">Sterling</option>
<option value="Suburu">Suburu</option>
<option value="Suzuki">Suzuki</option>
<option value="Toyota">Toyota</option>
<option value="Volkswagon">Volkswagon</option>
<option value="Volvo">Volvo</option>
<option value="Yugo">Yugo</option>
<option value="Other">Other</option>
</select>
</td>
</tr>
```

```
<tr valign="baseline">
<td align="right">Horsepower:</td>
<td nowrap colspan="3">
<input type="text" name="horsepower" size="6" maxlength="3">
hp
</td>
</tr>
<tr valign="baseline">
<td align="right">Cylinders:</td>
<td nowrap colspan="3">
<input type="radio" name="cylinders" value="4" checked>
4  
<input type="radio" name="cylinders" value="6">
6  
<input type="radio" name="cylinders" value="8">
8  
<input type="radio" name="cylinders" value="12">
12
</td>
</tr>
</table>
</form>
</body>
```

```
</html>

<html>
<head>
<title>Insert Car</title>
<script language="JavaScript">
function objectTag() {
```

After the standard opening tags, there is a script language tag that identifies the upcoming code as JavaScript. The `objectTag()` function is then initiated and the opening bracket ({) is added.

```
var theForm = document.forms[0];
```

As a matter of convenience, place the form from the user interface in a variable called *theForm*. This will save you from having to explicitly declare the form every time you want to reference it. It is much easier to say `theForm.horsepower.value` than to have to type in document.forms[0].horsepower.value. Each time you eliminate some typing, it not only saves time, it cuts down on bugs as well.

```
var model = theForm.model.options[theForm.model.selectedIndex].value;
```

You need to set three variables to hold the values that have been set as attributes of the Car object. The first is the Model, so set a variable named *model* and set the selected value from the form as the value of the variable. To do this with a drop-down box, you can get the value of a particular selection by treating the Options list as an array and calling options[*x*] where *x* is the index of the selection. Since you won't know which index has been selected, however, you can use a little trick to set the selectedIndex to use as the index of the options array.

```
var horsepower = theForm.horsepower.value;
```

The next variable is the Horsepower attribute and it is just text, so you can simply call its value.

```
var cylinders;
  for (var i=0; i < theForm.cylinders.length; i++) {
            if (theForm.cylinders[i].checked) {
                cylinders = theForm.cylinders[i].value;
                break;
                }
```

The Cylinders value must be determined by iterating through the Cylinders radio button collection. The preceding routine looks at each radio button in the group and sees if it is checked. When the checked button is found, the Cylinders variable is set to the value of that button and the routine breaks.

```
var attributes = "";
  attributes += ' model="' + model + '"';
  attributes += ' horsepower="' + horsepower + '"';
  attributes += ' cylinders="' + cylinders + '"';
```

One final variable, *attributes*, is set up to hold the string that will become the attributes of the tag. Since they are all strings at this point, you can simply build up the *attributes* variable by concatenating each piece of the string.

```
return "<CAR" + attributes + ">";
}
```

Finally, add the return that sends the whole thing to the insertion point on your page.

Save the file again as car.htm and place it in the Custom folder underneath the Dreamweaver Objects folder. When you restart Dreamweaver or reload your extensions, you will see the Insert Car object on your palette. Create an 18×18 GIF file to serve as the icon and save it in the same directory as you did the SiteURL object.

That does it for the object side of things. The only problem is that there is no <CAR> tag in HTML. Unlike an <HR> tag or a <table> tag, Dreamweaver has no idea what to do with a <CAR> tag until you tell it. That's where the third-party tag comes in.

Third-Party Tags and XML

A third-party tag is an XML file that holds information about your tag so that Dreamweaver knows what to do with it. Inside this XML file is a tag called <tagspec> that tells Dreamweaver several pieces of information. <Tagspec> has the following attributes and options:

- ▶ **tag_name** A string that assigns the name of the tag that this file describes.

- ▶ **tag_type** Either "empty" or "nonempty", this attribute identifies whether the tag will contain content and require a closing tag (like a <table> tag) or not (like an <HR> tag).

- ▶ **render_content** Set to either true or false, this attribute indicates whether the content of the tag will be displayed. If set to false (the default), the tag's icon is displayed rather than its content.

- ▶ **content_model** Establishes valid placement and content for the tag in the document. Its options are as follows:

  - ▶ **block_model** Tags that appear only in the body node of a document and contain block-level tags such as <p>, <div>, <blockquote>, or <pre>.

  - ▶ **head_model** Tags that appear in the head.

  - ▶ **marker_model** Tags that can be placed anywhere in the document with no restrictions on content (used mostly for inline tags).

  - ▶ **script_model** Tags that can be placed anywhere in the document with no restrictions on content. Content is totally ignored by Dreamweaver, so this model is useful for server-side scripts and so on.

There are other options for defining more advanced tags, but these should get you started just fine. Following is the tag specification for the <CAR> tag:

```
<tagspec tag_name="car" tag_type="empty" content_model="marker_model"
icon="car_tag.gif" icon_width="68" icon_height="36"></tagspec>
```

This tag specification says that the type is an empty tag; it contains no information and does not require a closing tag. It is of the marker_model type and has a placeholder icon called car_tag.gif with the specified height and width. When Dreamweaver encounters this tag, it will now know enough about it to handle it both in the HTML code and on your design page with your custom icon.

Save this file to the Third Party Tags folder under Configuration in the Dreamweaver directory. Also save your icon GIF file, car_tag.gif, to this folder. Restart Dreamweaver.

Now you can place your cursor anywhere on your page and select the car object. After filling in the appropriate information in the user interface, the <CAR> tag appears with the attributes you selected. And on the page is your car_tag icon indicating the presence of a <CAR> tag.

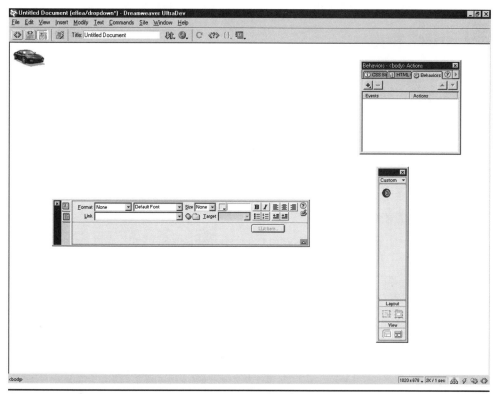

Figure 2-7   *The <CAR> tag icon appears once the object is applied*

Objects are one of the simpler extension types in Dreamweaver. More complex code manipulation can be accomplished with Behaviors, which we will look at next.

Behaviors

While the main purpose of objects is to place HTML code into the body of your pages, Behaviors go a step farther. Their purpose is to place JavaScript functions in the head of the page and add code to the body that calls those functions.

In this section, just to get the feel for it, you will construct a very simple Behavior that pops up a message box when a button is clicked or some other event occurs.

Behavior Functions

As with objects, building Behaviors is not difficult as long as you have a road map to follow. There are just a few functions that you need to implement.

canAcceptBehavior()

The `canAcceptBehavior()` function allows you to set prerequisites to the application of a Behavior. For instance, if the code you intend to implement moves a layer on the page, it would be necessary for there to be a layer on the page on which the Behavior code could operate. It doesn't make any sense to apply a Behavior that operates on a layer if there is no layer, and it may even cause problems to do so. You can insert code into this function that checks for any number of conditions and returns true only if the conditions are satisfied. If there are no preconditions to the application of your Behavior, you can just return true from the function.

behaviorFunction()

The `behaviorFunction()` function is responsible for identifying the code that is returned to the head of your page. You will see in the upcoming discussion that the function you want to insert into your page is defined in the Behavior. The `behaviorFunction()` returns that function's name so that the Behavior knows what code to insert.

applyBehavior()

The `applyBehavior()` function attaches a call to your function to an event in the HTML of your page. It is responsible for using information collected from the Behavior's user interface and formatting into the action that will occur when a button is clicked or a page is loaded.

inspectBehavior()

The `inspectBehavior()` function performs the same function as an object's Property Inspector. It collects the properties of an applied Behavior and repopulates the user interface so that it can be edited and reapplied.

initializeUI()

The `intializeUI()` function is called as soon as the Behavior is called. It performs whatever function you require to set up your user interface, such as populating a list box with values or setting the cursor's focus to a particular text box. Technically, this function is not a part of the Behavior API. It is just a custon JavaScript function that sets up the user interface and is called by the onLoad event of the body of the Behavioir's interface. It is a popular way to do this, though, so it's included here.

The BUDAlert Behavior

In order to get a feel for things, let's build a simple Behavior that pops up a JavaScript alert box when an event occurs. Remember that it is not the events that you are concerned about programming, it is the actions. Events are predefined. Your Behavior will apply the actions that you define to one of the predefined events that are available.

NOTE

You may be wondering about the name BUDAlert. Our UltraDev Web site is called Basic UltraDev and can be found at http://www.basic-ultradev.com. We often name extensions and variables after our site using the BUD abbreviation.

As always, the logical first step when creating an extension is to construct the final code that you need to implement outside of the extension. In this case, you'll need a JavaScript function that accepts a text message and displays it in an alert box:

```
function BUD_alert(message) {
    alert(unescape(message))
    }
```

This function takes a text message that is passed in, unescapes it, and displays it in a JavaScript alert box. The unescape function is used to be sure that the function properly displays any characters that the end user may pass in. The user's input is escaped to encode characters like double quotes, and it is then unescaped to decode it to its original form for display. Without this piece, many combinations of characters would display in unpredictable ways.

The second part of your code it the actual function call that will reside somewhere in the body of the page:

```
BUD_Alert("some message")
```

Now that these pieces are in place, you simply need to plug them into your Behavior and teach it how you want them applied. Here is the code for the complete Behavior; an explanation follows the code.

```html
<html>
<head>
<title>BUD Alert</title>
<meta http-equiv="Content-Type" content="text/html; charset=iso-8859-1">
<script language="JavsScript">
function BUD_alert(message) {
    alert(unescape(message))
    }
function canAcceptBehavior(){
    return true;
    }
function behaviorFunction(){
    return BUD_alert;
    }
    function applyBehavior(){
    var message
    message = escape(document.theForm.messagetext.value)
    return "BUD_alert('" + message + "')";
    }
function inspectBehavior(msgStr){
var messageArray = getTokens(msgStr,"()'");
var message = messageArray[1];
document.theForm.messagetext.value = unescape(message)
}
function initializeUI(){
    document.theForm.messagetext.focus()
    }
</script>
</head>
<body bgcolor="#FFFFFF" text="#000000" onLoad="initializeUI()">
<form name="theForm" method="post" action="">
  <font face="Arial, Helvetica, sans-serif"><b>Alert Text:</b></font>
  <input type="text" name="messagetext" size="50">
</form>
</body>
</html>
```

```
<html>
<head>
<title>BUD Alert</title>
<meta http-equiv="Content-Type" content="text/html; charset=iso-8859-1">
<script language="JavaScript">
function BUD_alert(message) {
     alert(unescape(message))
     }
```

After the initial <html> and <head> tags, insert an opening script tag and identify the scripting language as JavaScript. Next, insert the function that you wrote. This is the function that will be inserted into the head of your page when the Behavior is applied:

```
function canAcceptBehavior(){
     return true;
     }
```

Since this Behavior has no prerequisites, you can just return true from the canAcceptBehavior() function.

```
function behaviorFunction(){
     return BUD_alert;
     }
```

The behaviorFunction() function will control what function is returned to the page. Since there is only one function in this behavior, return the BUDAlert function:

```
function applyBehavior(){
     var message
     message = escape(document.theForm.messagetext.value)
     return "BUD_alert('" + message + "')";
     }
```

The applyBehavior() function is responsible for collecting your user's input, formatting it into an action, and applying it to the event that your user has selected. It works in conjunction with the behaviorFunction() function, with one returning the head function and the other returning the action. In this Behavior, the applyBehavior() function sets up a variable to hold the message that you want to pass. It then gets input from a form field on the user interface and escapes it to handle any odd characters. Finally, it formats that message variable into a string that will call the function from the event to which it is applied.

```
function inspectBehavior(msgStr){
var messageArray = getTokens(msgStr,"()'");
var message = messageArray[1];
document.theForm.messagetext.value = unescape(message)
}
```

The `inspectBehavior()` function does the opposite of `applyBehavior()`:
it uses the `getTokens()` function to strip out the message string that was applied. The
`getTokens()` function accepts two parameters: the string to parse and a list of the
characters to treat as separators. The function returns an array of tokens, or text blocks.
In this case, the first text block is the actual function name `BUD_Alert`. The second
block in the array is the message text. Since that is the piece that you need to access, you
can set `messageArray[1]` to the message variable. Since arrays start at an index of
0, the [1] index will return the second text block. You can then unescape that text and
set it to the text box on the user interface, and the user can edit and reapply it.

```
function initializeUI(){
     document.theForm.messagetext.focus()
     }
</script>
```

The `initializeUI()` function does whatever work it necessary to properly
display your HTML user interface. In this case, you simply need to set the cursor focus
to the `messagetext` box on your form, which is called theForm in the example.

```
</head>
<body bgcolor="#FFFFFF" text="#000000" onLoad="initializeUI()">
<form name="theForm" method="post" action="">
  <font face="Arial, Helvetica, sans-serif"><b>Alert Text:</b></font>
  <input type="text" name="messagetext" size="50">
</form>
</body>
</html>
```

The HTML portion of the Behavior is your user interface—in this case just a form
with a text box on it. Notice that there is no Submit button; Dreamweaver's Behavior
infrastructure will handle that.

Once you have your Behavior completed, you can save it to the Behaviors/Actions folder
in Dreamweaver's configuration directory. It will then become available as a Behavior

Figure 2-8   *Fill in the text you want the BUD_Alert behavior to display*

and can be applied as long as the prerequisites in your `canApplyBehavior()` function exist.

To apply this Behavior, select any object on your page or the page itself and choose the BUDAlert Behavior from the Plus (+) menu of the Behaviors palette. When the user interface appears, shown in Figure 2-8, fill in the text that you want alerted and click OK. In the Behaviors palette, select which of the object's available events you want to trigger your Behavior's action.

Behaviors are really quite straightforward. No matter how complex your user interface and functions get, they will always be implemented within this set of functions. The basic functionality remains the same: accept input from a user interface, format it, apply it as an action, and parse the action back into the user interface so that it can be edited.

A More Complex Behavior

Just about anything that you can do in client-side JavaScript can be turned into a Behavior. As an example, this next Behavior is a production Behavior from one of the most prolific extension writers around, Massimo Foti. This Behavior demonstrates two additional levels of complexity. First, the more advanced functions that Behaviors can perform, and second, many of the advanced coding techniques that can be used to make Behaviors more robust in a cross-platform environment.

Focus Field

The Focus Field extension serves a very simple but very important purpose. It allows you to identify in which form field you wish the cursor to appear when the page loads. This is a feature that is often overlooked by programmers, but it is a sign of a well-designed site if you care enough about your users' experience to address these kinds of details.

As always, it is the final code that is our first concern. Having code that is tested in and of itself is the first step to writing any extension. So, consider what the final code will look like in your page once the Focus Field extension has been applied:

```
<html>
<head>
<title>Focus Field Test</title>
<meta http-equiv="Content-Type" content="text/html; charset=iso-8859-1">
<script language="JavaScript">
<!--
function MM_findObj(n, d) { //v4.0
  var p,i,x;
  if(!d) d=document; if((p=n.indexOf("?"))>0&&parent.frames.length) {
    d=parent.frames[n.substring(p+1)].document; n=n.substring(0,p);}
  if(!(x=d[n])&&d.all) x=d.all[n]; for (i=0;!x&&i<d.forms.length;i++)
x=d.forms[i][n];
  for(i=0;!x&&d.layers&&i<d.layers.length;i++)
x=MM_findObj(n,d.layers[i].document);
  if(!x && document.getElementById) x=document.getElementById(n); return x;
}
function tmt_focusField(fieldName){
      var fieldObj = MM_findObj(fieldName);
      if(fieldObj){
            fieldObj.focus();
            fieldObj.select();

}
//-->
</script>
</head>
<body bgcolor="#FFFFFF" text="#000000" onLoad="tmt_focusField('username')">
<form name="login_form" method="post" action="">
  <input type="text" name="username">
  <input type="text" name="password">
  <input type="text" name="confirm">
</form>
</body>
</html>
```

This is the source code for a simple HTML page that has a form and three text boxes on it. It is the kind of form that you might use to collect a username and password and then confirm the password for a new registrant to your site. In fact, the text boxes are named username, password, and confirm.

When a user comes to this page, it is most likely that he will enter a username first, so you will want the cursor to move directly to that text box ready for entry when the page loads. Running the Focus Field Behavior on the page allows you to choose the text box that will receive focus. Notice in Figure 2-9 that you are given a very simple, plain English choice of the available elements on the page and in which forms they reside. This is done using a function called NiceNames() that we will look at later.

When you have selected the field that should receive the focus when your page loads, two sections of code are added to your page. First is the script section above the <head> tag that contains two functions, and second is the onLoad event that is appended to the <body> tag.

Focus Field Functions

The Focus Field extension adds two functions to your page. The primary function is actually inserted second, but let's look at it first.

tmt_focusField(fieldname)

The function that actually sets the focus to the chosen field is called tmt_focusField(), listed here:

```
function tmt_focusField(fieldName){
      var fieldObj = MM_findObj(fieldName);
      if(fieldObj){
            fieldObj.focus();
            fieldObj.select();
```

The tmt_focusField() function accepts the name of a field as a parameter. It then declares the variable *fieldobj* and sets its value to the return value of the second function, MM_findobj(), which also accepts the passed in field name as a parameter. If that field is located by MM_findobj(), (that is, if *fieldobj* is true, or has a value) then that field is given the focus and selected for input.

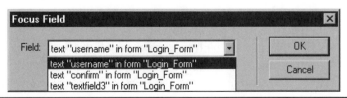

Figure 2-9 *The Focus Field user interface lets you pick from the available text boxes on your page*

MM_findobj(n,d)

MM_findobj() is a Macromedia function. It is found in the JavaScript file MM_findobj.js. This function accepts two parameters; a unique object name and the DOM in which to search for the object. The DOM parameter is used for recursion and is not normally passed in. You will notice that in the code we are discussing, only the fieldname (the n parameter) is passed in. A quick look at the function itself shows how this is handled:

```
function MM_findObj(n, d) {
    var p,i,x;
    if(!d) d=document;
    if((p=n.indexOf("?"))>0&&parent.frames.length) {
        d=parent.frames[n.substring(p+1)].document;
        n=n.substring(0,p);
    }
    if(!(x=d[n])&&d.all) x=d.all[n];
    for (i=0;!x&&i<d.forms.length;i++)
        x=d.forms[i][n];
    for(i=0;!x&&d.layers&&i<d.layers.length;i++)
        x=MM_findObj(n,d.layers[i].document);
    if(!x && document.getElementById) x=document.getElementById(n);
    return x;
}
```

Notice the third line of the function:

```
If(!d) d=document;
```

If no DOM information is passed in, the second function parameter is set to the current document, and it is the document that is searched for the named object.

The next section of code is what makes the MM_findobj() function so powerful. Instead of passing in a simple object name, like textfield1, you can append a frame target to the object name using ? as a delimiter. So calling MM_findobj(textfield1?topframe) searches the frame called topframe for the object called textfield1. By allowing this, you can set the focus to a form object that exists in a separate frame from that in which the function is called. This is done by determining if the ? exists in the parameter and then splitting off the frame that is to be searched. If the ? does not exist in the parameter, the base document is searched.

Once the object name and the search area are defined, the function iterates through the elements in that search area looking for a match for the object name. During this process, the `MM_find obj()` function calls itself in a recursive fashion to search all of the available layers in the document. During this process, the index of the layer being searched is passed in as the second parameter, thus explaining its definition in the function.

Once the search is completed, assuming that the selected object is located, its location is passed back to the calling function, `tmt_focusField()`, in this case.

The onLoad Event

The second piece of code that is added to your page is the onLoad event of the `<body>` tag.

```
<body bgcolor="#FFFFFF" text="#000000" onLoad="tmt_focusField('username')">
```

The onLoad event calls the `tmt_focusField()` function and passes in the object name that you selected when the Behavior was inserted. That object name is then passed to the `MM_findobj()` function where the object is located and passed back to the `tmt_focusField()` function. The focus is then set to that field, and the page is displayed.

You can see that this is a much more powerful implementation of this simple idea than just hard-coding the focus method directly into the onLoad event of the body. It allows for the named object to reside in a layer on the page or in a separate frame altogether. The latest version of the `MM_findobj()` function (version 4.01) even works in Netscape 6.

Understanding what needs to happen in the final code is absolutely necessary, but that is just the first step. Constructing a Behavior that outputs this code to you page is the tricky part.

The Focus Field Behavior

Take a look at the code for the Focus Field Behavior:

```
<script language="JavaScript" src="MM_findObj.js"></script>
<script language="JavaScript">
//****************** BEHAVIOR FUNCTION ********************
function tmt_focusField(fieldName){
    var fieldObj = MM_findObj(fieldName);
```

```
        if(fieldObj){
                fieldObj.focus();
                fieldObj.select();
        }
}
//****************** API ********************
function canAcceptBehavior(){
        var elementsArray = getAllObjectRefs("NS
4.0","INPUT/TEXT","TEXTAREA","INPUT/PASSWORD");
        return (elementsArray.length > 0);
}
function behaviorFunction(){
        return "MM_findObj,tmt_focusField";
}
function applyBehavior() {
        var elementsArray,field1Index,field1Name,spaceKiller,errorMsg;
        var argString = "";
        elementsArray = getAllObjectRefs("NS 4.0",
"INPUT/TEXT","TEXTAREA","INPUT/PASSWORD");
        if(elementsArray.length > 0){
                field1Index = findObject("THE_FIELD").selectedIndex;
                if(elementsArray[field1Index].indexOf(REF_UNNAMED) != 0){
                argString += "'" + getNameFromRef(elementsArray[field1Index]) + "'";
                        return "tmt_focusField(" + argString + ")";
                }
                else{
                        return "\n" + "Can only affect *named* text fields. Please
click Cancel, and name your text field using the Property Inspector";
                }
        }
        else{
                return "\n" + "No text fields found inside the document\nThe Action
will not be added to your document";
        }
}
function inspectBehavior(enteredStr){
        if(enteredStr){
                var argArray,elementsArray,selectMenu,elementFound;
                argArray = extractArgs(enteredStr);
                elementsArray = getAllObjectRefs("NS 4.0",
"INPUT/TEXT","TEXTAREA","INPUT/PASSWORD");
                selectMenu = findObject("THE_FIELD");
                for(var i=0;i<selectMenu.options.length;i++){
                if(getNameFromRef(elementsArray[i]) == argArray[1]){
                        selectMenu.selectedIndex = i;
```

```
                    elementFound = true;
                                break;
                }
                }
                if(!elementFound){
                        alert(argArray[1] + " could not be found, it may have been
renamed or deleted")
                }
        }
}
//**************** UI FUNCTIONS  *****************
function populateSelect(formElement,itemsArrays){//1.7m
        var theSelect;
        theSelect = findObject(formElement);
        theSelect.options.length = 0;
        for (var i=0; i<itemsArrays.length; i++){
                theSelect.options[i] = new Option(itemsArrays[i]);
        }
        theSelect.selectedIndex = 0;
}
function initializeUI(){
        var niceNamesArray;
        niceNamesArray = niceNames(getAllObjectRefs("NS
4.0","INPUT/TEXT","TEXTAREA","INPUT/PASSWORD"),TYPE_Text);
        populateSelect("THE_FIELD",niceNamesArray);
}
</script>
<style type="text/css">
.longTextField {  width: 230px}
</style>
</head>
<body onLoad="initializeUI()">
<form name="theForm" action="">
  <table border="0">
    <tr>
      <td nowrap valign="top">Field:</td>
      <td valign="top">
        <select name="THE_FIELD" class="longTextField">
        </select>
      </td>
    </tr>
  </table>
</form>
</body>
</html>
```

Focus Field Behavior Functions

Just as we did with the BUDAlert Behavior, we'll look at each of the functions that make up the Behavior. We will then offer some general comments about this Behavior.

```
//****************** BEHAVIOR FUNCTION *********************
function tmt_focusField(fieldName){
    var fieldObj = MM_findObj(fieldName);
    if(fieldObj){
        fieldObj.focus();
        fieldObj.select();
    }
}
```

The Behavior function section identifies the Behavior or Behaviors that will be inserted into the page. In this case, you will be inserting two functions, but the other one (the MM_findobj<> function) is defined in the MM_finsobj.js file that is included by reference at the beginning of the code.

```
function canAcceptBehavior(){
    var elementsArray = getAllObjectRefs("NS
4.0","INPUT/TEXT","TEXTAREA","INPUT/PASSWORD");
    return (elementsArray.length > 0);
```

The canAcceptBehavior() function checks for the existence of objects that can accept focus. It uses the getAllObjectRefs() function and passes in the DOM that you are using (NS 4.0) and the object types you are searching for (text boxes, text areas, and password boxes). The function returns true and continues processing if any of these are found, or it returns false, aborting the Behavior, if none are found.

```
function behaviorFunction(){
    return "MM_findObj,tmt_focusField";
}
```

The behaviorFunction() function is responsible for actually determining what functions are sent to the page. In this case, two functions are designated to be returned when this Behavior is applied.

```
function applyBehavior() {
      var elementsArray,field1Index,field1Name,spaceKiller,errorMsg;
      var argString = "";
      elementsArray = getAllObjectRefs("NS 4.0",
"INPUT/TEXT","TEXTAREA","INPUT/PASSWORD");
      if(elementsArray.length > 0){
            field1Index = findObject("THE_FIELD").selectedIndex;
            if(elementsArray[field1Index].indexOf(REF_UNNAMED) != 0){
            argString += "'" + getNameFromRef(elementsArray[field1Index]) + "'";
                  return "tmt_focusField(" + argString + ")";
            }
            else{
                  return "\n" + "Can only affect *named* text fields. Please
click Cancel, and name your text field using the Property Inspector";
            }
      }
      else{
            return "\n" + "No text fields found inside the document\nThe Action
will not be added to your document";
      }
}
```

The `applyBehavior()` function takes care of actually applying the designated
functions to your page. While the `canAcceptBehavior()` function determines
that there are the proper types of fields on the page, this function actually gets all
of them and stuffs them into an array so that they can be checked against the object
name you are looking for. Once that array is built, the item within it that matches
the element you are searching for is pulled out. That element is tested to see that
it is named. If it is named, it is added to the argument list, and if not, the user is
notified that this Behavior can only use named objects and the Behavior is aborted.
The argument string is appended to the function name, and this string is returned
to the onLoad event of the <body> tag on your page.

```
function inspectBehavior(enteredStr){
      if(enteredStr){
            var argArray,elementsArray,selectMenu,elementFound;
            argArray = extractArgs(enteredStr);
            elementsArray = getAllObjectRefs("NS 4.0",
"INPUT/TEXT","TEXTAREA","INPUT/PASSWORD");
            selectMenu = findObject("THE_FIELD");
            for(var i=0;i<selectMenu.options.length;i++){
            if(getNameFromRef(elementsArray[i]) == argArray[1]){
```

```
                            selectMenu.selectedIndex = i;
                elementFound = true;
                        break;
            }
            }
            if(!elementFound){
                alert(argArray[1] + " could not be found, it may have been
renamed or deleted")
            }
        }
    }
}
```

Again, the `inspectBehavior()` function does very much the opposite of the `applyBehavior()` function. It first accepts a parameter of the onLoad event string. It then checks to see that this string exists. An anomaly in Dreamweaver can cause an empty string to be returned to an `inspectBehavior()` function, so always check to see that the string is not empty.

Next, the entered string is parsed to retrieve the field name. The `extractArgs()` function returns an array that will include the function name as the first index and the field name as the second. The page is again checked for the eligible element types, and they are collected into an array to be checked against the field name, which is index [1] of the `argArray`. If the element is found, the Behavior's UI is set to that element; if not, the user is notified that the proper element has been deleted from the page.

```
function populateSelect(formElement,itemsArrays){//1.7m
    var theSelect;
    theSelect = findObject(formElement);
    theSelect.options.length = 0;
    for (var i=0; i<itemsArrays.length; i++){
        theSelect.options[i] = new Option(itemsArrays[i]);
    }
    theSelect.selectedIndex = 0;
}
function initializeUI(){
    var niceNamesArray;
    niceNamesArray = niceNames(getAllObjectRefs("NS
4.0","INPUT/TEXT","TEXTAREA","INPUT/PASSWORD"),TYPE_Text);
    populateSelect("THE_FIELD",niceNamesArray);
}
```

The actual Behavior function here is `initializeUI()`. The `populateSelect()` function is a helper function that populates the drop-down list on the user interface. It has been included here because of its usefulness and because it is called from the `initializeUI()` function.

When the Behavior is called, an array is built of all of the eligible elements that exist in the document. This time, though, the result of the `getAllobjectRefs()` is passed to a function called `nicenames()`. The `nicenames()` function is a Macromedia function that converts the rather ugly reference that is returned by the `getAllobjectRefs()` function into a very readable format, as you saw in Figure 2-9. This array is passed to the `populateSelect()` function, along with the name of the drop-down box on the user interface that you want populated with these object references. It is thus populated:

```
</script>
<style type="text/css">
.longTextField {  width: 230px}
</style>
</head>
<body onLoad="initializeUI()">
<form name="theForm" action="">
  <table border="0">
    <tr>
      <td nowrap valign="top">Field:</td>
      <td valign="top">
        <select name="THE_FIELD" class="longTextField">
        </select>
      </td>
    </tr>
  </table>
</form>
</body>
</html>
```

The remainder of the Behavior code is the HTML that makes up the user interface. It defines a table and a select box that will be populated with the values returned by `nicenames()`.

Some General Observations about Focus Field

There is a lot happening in the Focus Field Behavior; it is an excellent example of techniques that you can use to make your extensions more robust and stable. You must remember that the developers who use your extensions will do so on a number of platforms with a number of target browsers in mind. Here are some general observations about the way this extension is written that may help you in your development efforts.

▶ Note that this Behavior does not link to any Macromedia shared files. All of the code that is used by this Behavior is already loaded in memory by Dreamweaver so it can be called as if it were native to the current file. This feature is available for any JavaScript file that includes this comment inside it: //SHARE-IN-MEMORY=true. This is an undocumented feature that is available in Dreamweaver 4.0. Using it, you can call functions like `getNameFromRef()`, `extractAgs()`, and `nicenames()` without having to link to the relevant .js files.

▶ The only custom JavaScript routine that is used is the `populateselect()` function. There is a file class called ListCOntrolClass.js that is a Macromedia class to accomplish the same thing, but this method is less intimidating to the average user.

▶ The `MMfindobj()` function is important to allow the inspection of forms inside layers in Netscape Navigator and to work across frames easily. It is included by reference instead of being coded into the Behavior to make sure that the most recent version is always used.

▶ To create easy to use and robust Behaviors, using MM's `getAllObjectRefs()` routine is crucial. You can find additional information about it inside the docInfo.js file. When you call something like: `getAllObjectRefs("NS 4.0","INPUT/TEXT","TEXTAREA","INPUT/PASSWORD")`, Dreamweaver returns an array of NN 4 DOM references for all the text fields, text areas, and password fields available inside the current document, including any open frame. If you need a different kind of elements you can just change the arguments. For layers, use `getAllObjectRefs ("NS 4.0","LAYER")`; for images, use `getAllObjectRefs("NS 4.0","IMG")`.

As you can see, by simply changing this call, you can turn this Behavior into a very generic, reusable framework that you can use for form elements, images, layers, or other elements.

▶ You need to consider what kind of strings `getAllObjectRefs()` returns. Since you are dealing with the NN 4 DOM, you can get long and ugly strings returned. For example, a text field inside a layer will look like the following:

```
document.layers['LayerName'].document.formName.fieldName
```

If you pass this reference to `niceNames()` as the first argument and text as the second argument, you will get:

```
"text fieldName in form formName in layer LayerName"
```

This is exactly what you need to display a friendly reference to the user and is what was done inside the `initializeUI()` function of the example.

However, since the client-side script just needs the name of the form element, you can use the `getNameFromRef()` function. Call it like this:

```
getNameFromRef("document.layers['LayerName'].document.formName.fieldName");
```

and you will get "fieldName" as a return value.

When you are targeting elements across frames, `getAllObjectRefs()` will return an awful NN 4 DOM reference:

```
parent.frames['frameName']document.layers['LayerName'].document.formName.fieldName
```

But, if you pass this string to `getNameFromRef()`, you get:

```
textfield?mainFrame
```

This is exactly the format that your client-side `MM_findObj()` can handle.

▶ A benefit of using `MM_findObj()` on the client-side script is not only to make it work as a cross-browser "DOM equalizer," but also to easily target HTML elements across frames

What to Take Away from this Chapter

You can see that objects and Behaviors are extremely powerful extensions. While they are simpler in nature than some of what the rest of this book will cover, learning to write them correctly is of tremendous benefit to the extensionologist. They are the building blocks on which the more advanced extensions are based.

Once you have a handle on these simpler extensions, you should have an easier time understanding commands and Server Behaviors, which will be covered in upcoming chapters.

Exercises

1. Add a text element to the Car Object that will accept the model year of the car.

2. Alter the BUDAlert behavior so that it can accept its alert text from the end user at run time.

3. Pick another popular behavior extension and break its components down like was done to Focus Field in this chapter. Learn all you can about the Macromedia functions that are used in the behavior by finding them on your computer and reading the notes that come along with them.

Commands

Commands are perhaps the most powerful of the extensions, as they can perform powerful document and site manipulation and can be called from any other extension. Some of them appear on the Commands menu of Dreamweaver and include things like Clean Up HTML and Add/Remove Netscape Resize Fix. A command can add code to a page or manipulate code that's already on the page. You can manipulate HTML tags, JavaScript, server-side code, or virtually any sort of text or code that might be contained in a document. You can even create new documents and populate them with some predefined code on the fly.

Commands are only limited by your imagination and your JavaScript skills. When you look at a Web page in the Dreamweaver environment and say, "I wish I could do [blank] to the page," chances are good that you can make a command out of it. When you say, "I wish I could do [blank] to all pages in the site," that's a good time for a site-wide command.

Sometimes there is a fine line between Commands, Objects, and Behaviors, but no matter what you decide to do with your code, it's a good idea to know all of the possibilities open to you.

Using Commands

Commands that appear on the Commands menu are generally there to perform an action of some kind to your page or to a selected region of the page. For example, the Clean Up Word HTML command will scour your page for instances of MS Word–specific HTML and XML code and remove it.

This particular command is also configurable by the user with check boxes, as seen in Figure 3-1. By checking various attributes of the command, different actions will be performed on the document. These can be separate commands themselves, but they are all gathered into this one command file to perform the actions as a group. For example, one of the actions is Set bgcolor #FFFFFF, which sets the background to white. While that can be a command by itself, in this instance it is part of the group of functions that make up the Clean Up HTML from Word command. This grouping of commands together is a technique you can consider for your own command file.

The Clean Up HTML from Word command also shows the use of the multiple-tabbed interface, which has become quite popular in Dreamweaver extensions.

Commands can have attributes that a user can fill out, or they can run without any user interaction, as with the Apply Source Formatting command, which makes your HTML neat just by clicking it. Put some code on the page and then mess it up a little bit and try out the command. In Design view, it seems as if nothing has happened.

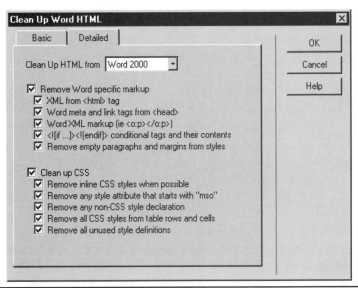

Figure 3-1   *The Clean Up HTML from Word command shows the use of check boxes and multiple tabs in a command*

No dialog box pops up, and no change is made to the page. In Code view, however, you'll see that the code has been arranged in a standard Dreamweaver format as if Dreamweaver had generated the code, with all the tables neatly arranged and indented.

The Command API

Like the other extensions, Dreamweaver command files have an Application Programming Interface (API). One difference, however, is that the functions are not required. If you do use functions, the programmer must define them and any return values that are needed. The command file can be called by accessing a command from the Commands menu, or it can be called with a dw.runCommand() or dw.popupCommand() function call. When the user chooses the Commands menu, Dreamweaver looks for the canAcceptCommand() function. If this function returns true, the rest of the command is shown in the menu and the user can choose it if he wants to. If the function returns false, the command is dimmed in the menu, thereby making it less confusing for the user. For example, a command that only works on a selected image would return false if an image isn't currently selected.

Next, the function receiveArguments() is called. If the runCommand() function passed any arguments to the command, they can be picked up in this function. For example, the Flash Button command takes an argument that is passed from the Flash Button Object file that calls the command.

The next optional function that Dreamweaver attempts to find is the `commandButtons()` function. If this function is defined, Dreamweaver will display the appropriate buttons that the programmer has defined. Each button needs to have a corresponding function assigned to it, so that when a user clicks a button, the function assigned to that button is fired off. If this function isn't defined, no buttons will be displayed in the command.

Next, Dreamweaver will look for a `<form>` tag in the body of the command file. If there is a `<form>` tag, Dreamweaver will then look for a `windowDimensions()` function. In that function, the programmer can define a size for the dialog box of the command. You shouldn't define this function unless you want the dialog box bigger than 640×480 pixels. If the function isn't defined, Dreamweaver will build the dialog box to the best size for the buttons defined. If there is no `<form>` tag, no dialog box is displayed.

Next, the user can make choices and fill out the form. If the user clicks a button, the corresponding function will be called. The command stays open until such time as the `window.close()` function is called. It is during this phase of the command that all of the document manipulation takes place. For example, in the Set Color Scheme command, the user can choose different combinations of colors, as shown in Figure 3-2. The color combinations are chosen from list boxes, and the color display of the fonts in the command interface change, but no change is made to the document. Only when the user clicks Apply do the changes occur to the document.

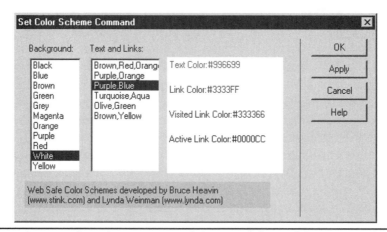

Figure 3-2 *The Set Color Scheme command shows good use of the commandButtons() function, with the Apply button*

Also, the dialog box remains in place until the user clicks OK. Only then is the `window.close()` function called and the dialog box is closed.

As you can see, a command is pretty flexible, in that there are no hard-and-fast rules about how they have to be built. You can choose to define any or all of the API functions or define your own functions.

Menu-Location=None

A command file is similar to the HTML files that we created for Objects and Behaviors. There are a few differences, however. For one, not every command has a corresponding menu item. If you look inside the Commands folder, you'll see quite a few commands that don't appear on the Commands menu. There are a couple ways you can use commands to enhance your other extensions. You can invoke a command with a `dw.runCommand()` function call or with the `dw.popupCommand()` function call. Simply put the following line as the first line in your Command file:

```
<!-- MENU-LOCATION=NONE -->
```

This is done for many reasons. Commands are more versatile than some of the other extensions like Inspectors, for instance. An Inspector must reside in a small interface to conform to the Macromedia standards. Frequently, you will have to invoke a command to display a larger interface for editing some code or attributes. If you look at the asp.js file in the Inspectors folder in UltraDev, for instance, you'll notice the `launchASPEditDialog()` function, which gets the selected object and then calls the `dw.popupCommand("EditContent")` to invoke a code editor for the ASP tag that was selected by the user. The ASP Property Inspector has only one button on it—the button that calls the command, as shown in Figure 3-3. You can do this in your own Property Inspectors, as well.

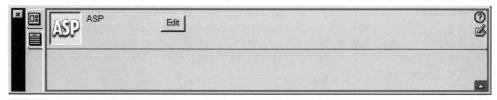

Figure 3-3 *The ASP Property Inspector in UltraDev shows the use of a command called from the Inspector*

TIP

As always, looking at existing code is a great way to learn how to apply the techniques to your own programming. The existing command files offer a wealth of information.

Another reason to apply the `<!-- MENU-LOCATION=NONE -->` directive is so that you can specify your own menu location from within an MXI file. MXI files will be dealt with in a later chapter, but if you are already making your own extensions you are probably familiar with them already. For example, you might have an extension that only appears in the right-click menu for an image. You can set the `<!-- MENU-LOCATION=NONE -->` directive and then specify the DWImageContext menu from within the MXI file.

Creating a Basic Command

Next, you'll create a very basic command to show you how to manipulate the document. This command will simply wrap any selected text or object with comment tags, so that you can freely comment on your HTML without leaving the design environment. You can also choose to "comment out" some text or an object while designing your site, which is useful for debugging. The code for the command is as follows:

```
<html>
<head>
<title>MakeComment</title>
<script language="javascript">
<!--
//global variables
var openTag = '<!--\n'
var closeTag = '\n-->';
function makeComment() {
// Get Selected text and wrap with comment tags
    var dom = dw.getDocumentDOM();//get the dom
    var sel = dom.getSelection();//get the selected text or object
    var wrapthis = dom.documentElement.outerHTML.substring(sel[0], sel[1]);
    wrapthis = openTag + wrapthis + closeTag;//wrap the selected text
    dw.getDocumentDOM().insertHTML(wrapthis);//insert into the document
    window.close();
    }
// -->
</script>
</head>
```

```
<body onLoad="makeComment()">
</body>
</html>
```

The code is fairly simple. First, you declare two variables for your open and close tags. Then you declare the makeComment() function, which is called from the body onLoad event of the extension. The makeComment() function simply gets the document Dom and acquires the selected text by using the offsets that were returned by the getSelection() method of the Dom and getting the outerHTML property. Finally, you just need to wrap the open and close tags around the selection and insert it back into the document.

If you save the extension in the Commands folder at this point as MakeComment.htm and restart UltraDev, you can apply it by making a selection on the page and then choosing MakeComment from the Commands menu. When you do this, any selected text will be collapsed into a comment tag. How are you going to uncomment the item now? Just write another command: StripCommentTags. Here is the code for that command:

```
<html>
<head>
<title>StripCommentTags</title>
<script language="javascript">
<!--
function stripComment() {
    // Get Selected comment and strip comment tags
    var doc = dw.getDocumentDOM(); //get the DOM
    var sel = doc.getSelection(); //get the selection
    var theNode = dw.offsetsToNode(sel[0],sel[1]);
    if(theNode.nodeType==Node.COMMENT_NODE) {
        sel=theNode.data;
        dw.getDocumentDOM().insertHTML(sel);
    }
    window.close();
}
// -->
</script>
</head>
<body onLoad="stripComment()">
</body>
</html>
```

This command works in a similar fashion to the MakeComment command. However, after getting the selection, the command first checks to see if the selected node is a comment node. If it is a comment, it gets the *data* property of the node. The data property contains the area that's inside of the tags in *comment* nodes and *text* nodes. It's similar to the `innerHTML` property of the *element* nodes. After getting the data property, you then write the HTML out to the document without the comment tags.

These techniques can be used to add server-side code as well. You could easily modify the MakeComment command to insert any of the server markup shown in Table 3-1 or to insert code before and after the selected text by changing the openTag and closeTag variables.

Buttons in Command Files

Another Command file feature worth mentioning is the ability of the programmer to define the buttons for the interface on the fly—making them contextual and dependent on conditions that you can set up programmatically. One good example of this technique is the Add/Remove Netscape Resize Fix command. In that command, the button shown in the interface depends upon whether or not the user has already applied the command to the page. If the command has been applied, the user is shown the Remove button; if the command hasn't been applied yet, the user is shown the Add button. You can easily adapt your MakeComment/StripComment commands to share a single interface by using this technique.

openTag	closeTag
`<% =`	`%>`
`<%Response.Write("`	`")%>`
`<cfoutput>`	`</cfoutput>`
`<%try{`	`}catch(java.lang.Exception e){;}%>`
`<%If Session("Username")<>"" Then %>`	`<%End If%>`
`<cfif IsDefined("Session.Username")>`	`</cfif>`
`<%if(MM_offset != 0)%>`	`<%}%>`

Table 3-1   *Possible Variations on the MakeComment Command*

```
<html>
<head>
<title>Make/Strip Comment</title>
<script language="javascript">
<!--
//global variables
function commandButtons() {
  var retArr;
  // Include only buttons that make sense for the current selection.
  if (isComment()){
    retArr = new Array("Strip Comment", "stripComment();",
                       "Cancel","window.close()");
  } else {
    retArr = new Array("Make Comment","makeComment();",
                       "Cancel","window.close()");
  }
  return retArr;
}
function makeComment() {
    // Get Selected text and wrap with comment tags
    var openTag = '<!--\n'
    var closeTag = '\n-->';
    var doc = dw.getDocumentDOM();
    var sel = doc.getSelection();
    var wrapthis = doc.documentElement.outerHTML.substring(sel[0], sel[1]);
    wrapthis = openTag + wrapthis + closeTag;
    dw.getDocumentDOM().insertHTML(wrapthis);
    window.close();
    }
function stripComment() {
    // Get Selected comment and strip comment tags
    var doc = dw.getDocumentDOM();
    var sel = doc.getSelection();
    var theNode = dw.offsetsToNode(sel[0],sel[1]);
    if(theNode.nodeType==Node.COMMENT_NODE) {
        sel=theNode.data;
        dw.getDocumentDOM().insertHTML(sel);
    }
    window.close();
    }
function isComment() {
    var doc = dw.getDocumentDOM();
    var theNode = doc.getSelectedNode();
```

```
      if(theNode.nodeType == Node.COMMENT_NODE) {
          return true;
      }else{
          return false;

      }
}
// -->
</script>
</head>
<body></body>
</html>
```

Here's an explanation of what's happening in this code: the `commandButtons()` function is recognized by Dreamweaver as a built-in command function. DW expects to be returned as an array of buttons with corresponding function calls. You have to set up an array so that it is structured as button, function, button, function, and so on. You can have as many buttons as you need, but you should keep them to a minimum. The array is programmatically triggered by the `isComment()` function, which simply returns a true or false value after checking to see if the selected node is a comment node. If it is, the buttons will be labeled Strip Comment and Cancel. If the selection isn't a comment, the buttons will be labeled Make Comment and Cancel.

The remaining two functions in the command file are the identical functions that you've seen already in the two previous commands. Save this file in the Commands folder now as CommentCommands.htm and restart Dreamweaver. You can then test it out by selecting some text or object on the page and choosing CommentCommands from the Commands menu. Notice that the Make Comment button is visible, as shown in the following illustration.

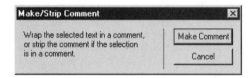

If you select the newly created comment at this point and apply the command again, the button will magically change to Strip Comment, as shown in the next illustration.

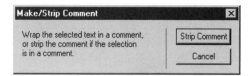

Using Regular Expressions in Commands

Regular expressions (RegExps) are a powerful feature of JavaScript that you'll
have to become thoroughly familiar with if you expect to become proficient at
building extensions for Dreamweaver. A simple RegExp can perform powerful
document manipulation and site-wide document manipulation. Take a look at
this example:

```
var theDom = dw.getDocumentDOM();
var theDoc = theDom.documentElement.outerHTML;
theDoc = theDoc.replace(/(<\/?)layer([^>]*>)/gi,"$1div$2")
dw.getDocumentDOM().outerHTML = theDoc;
```

The *replace* method of the RegExp object is used to find all instances of the
<layer> tag. The question mark (?) following the slash character (/) means that
the slash is optional, which will match opening and closing layer tags. Also, the
tag can contain specific attributes because you are using the negated character
class [^>]*that will search for all characters up to a closing > character. The *gi* is
shorthand for global (g) and case-insensitive (i) search. Finally, the string that you
are using for the replacement string uses the grouping levels of the search expression
(the parentheses). The $1 and $2 expressions are variables that contain whatever is
within the parentheses after the match. You place the "div" between the two
variables to
take the place of the "layer." A list of the regular expression special characters
is shown in Table 3-2.

One of the best places to practice the use of regular expressions is the Find/Replace
dialog box in Dreamweaver. In this box you can put your complex RegExps and do
site-wide searching and replacing of specific text. For example, if you were to enter
the following in the Find/Replace dialog

```
<a\s*href\s*=\s*\"http:\/\/[^"]*\">[^<]*<\/a>
```

Character	What It Means
\	For regular characters, it indicates that the next character is a special directive. For special characters, it indicates that the following character should be taken literally.
^	Matches the beginning of the string.
$	Matches the end of the string.
*	Matches the preceding character 0 or more times.
+	Matches the preceding character 1 or more times.
?	Matches the preceding character 0 or 1 times.
.	Matches any single character except the newline character. A commonly used expression is .*, meaning "zero or more of any character."
(x)	Matches x and remembers the match.
x|y	Matches either x or y'.
{n}	Matches exactly n occurrences of the preceding character.
{n,}	Matches at least n occurrences of the preceding character.
{n,m}	Matches at least n and at most m occurrences of the preceding character.
[xyz] or [A–Z]	A character set. Matches any one of the enclosed characters.
[^xyz] or [^0–9]	A negated or complemented character set. That is, it matches anything that is not enclosed in the brackets. You can specify a range of characters by using a hyphen.
[\b]	Matches a backspace.
\b	Matches a word boundary, such as a space or a newline character.
\B	Matches a nonword boundary.
\cX	Where X is a control character. Matches a control character in a string.
\d	Matches a digit character.
\D	Matches any nondigit character.
\f	Matches a form-feed.
\n	Matches a line feed.
\r	Matches a carriage return.
\s	Matches a single white space character, including space, tab, form feed, and line feed.
\S	Matches a single character other than white space.

Table 3-2   *Regular Expression Special Characters*

Character	What It Means
\t	Matches a tab.
\v	Matches a vertical tab.
\w	Matches any alphanumeric character including the underscore.
\W	Matches any nonword character.
\n	A back reference to the last substring matching the n parenthetical in the regular expression (counting left parentheses).
\ooctal	Where \ooctal is an octal escape value. Allows you to embed ASCII codes into regular expressions.
\xhex	Where \xhex is a hexadecimal escape value. Allows you to embed ASCII codes into regular expressions.

Table 3-2 *Regular Expression Special Characters* (continued)

you would be able to find all links in your site. Enter this RegExp:

```
<\/?font[^>]*>
```

and you will find all opening AND closing font tags. The following RegExp

```
<img\s*([^>]*)>
```

will find all instances of an image tag. If you want to add a `border="0"` to each instance of an image tag in your site, you could replace the above with this:

```
<img $1 border="0">
```

In this example, the attributes of the image tag are "remembered" by the regular expression and stored in the variable `$1`. Then you simply replace the image tag with a new one, leaving the attributes intact but adding a border attribute of 0. When writing your own regular expressions in an extension file, keep in mind that the preceding expression will *add* a border attribute whether there is one there already or not.

Using regular expressions is a far superior method to using a regular text based search because you can search with "fuzzy" searches that don't match text exactly. Needless to say, regular expressions are a big part of Dreamweaver extensibility, and you can do more serious extension work if you know how to create regular expressions. For UltraDev extensibility, regular expressions are part of the core functionality of Server Behaviors.

Making History Commands

One of the most powerful features of Dreamweaver is the ability to take a group of actions that were performed on the page and replay them using the History palette. Even better, you can take this same group of actions and make them into a command by selecting the history steps that you want to replay and then clicking Save (the floppy disk image) or choosing Save As Command from the contextual menu of the History palette. This can save you a lot of time—not only in your Web page creation, but also in your extension development.

When you save a set of history steps as a command, the command automatically appears on the Commands menu; it also appears as an HTML file in the Commands folder. For example, if you insert a table with 2 rows and 3 columns, with width set to 100%, cellspacing set to 0, and cellpadding set to 0, you could save the action as a command. You would then be able to run this from the Commands menu. If you have a site where certain table sizes are being used frequently, you could even have a whole group of these in a submenu. If you look at the command that is created, you'll see that the table is being inserted with a simple call to the DW API. The `runCommand()` function is actually run from the `onLoad()` event of the body. The extraneous comments and the actual table code produced by Dreamweaver have been removed in this example so the code is easier to read.

```
function runCommand()
    {
    dw.getDocumentDOM().insertHTML('[table code here]', false);
    }
```

That is about as basic as you can get. But what if you want to increase the complexity of the command? You can do that too and save as many history steps as you want into a command. For example, add a border color of #9999CC, a bgcolor of #CCCCCC and a center alignment to the same table. The command file will then have the following lines added to it:

```
// Set Attribute: bordercolor, #9999CC
dw.getDocumentDOM().setAttributeWithErrorChecking('bordercolor', '#9999CC');
// Set Bg Color: #CCCCCC
dw.getDocumentDOM().setAttributeWithErrorChecking('bgcolor', '#CCCCCC');
// Set Alignment: CENTER
dw.getDocumentDOM().setAttributeWithErrorChecking('align', 'CENTER');
```

This is just a basic exercise, but you can expand upon the principle and build your own complex commands using these techniques. Since the command files that are generated are HTML and JavaScript, they can be modified to include whatever functionality you want. For instance, in the preceding example, you could pop up a dialog box to allow the user to choose the bgcolor attribute of the table.

Copying a History Command to the Clipboard

History commands have many uses, and once you start using them you will find all sorts of shortcuts that will help you in your extension writing. Did you know that you can save a history command to the clipboard and reapply it to the page? For example, say you wanted to apply bold and italic font attributes to some text. You could apply it to one word, then go to the History palette and select both history steps. By using the contextual menu (right-click on a PC and Control-click on a Mac), you can save the commands to the clipboard so that the same steps can be applied to other text. After saving the steps, you can simply highlight some text and click Paste, and your steps will be replayed on the current selection.

Replaying the History is only the beginning. Once you understand the implications of the technique, you'll see that you can copy History commands and paste them into Notepad or any other text editor of your choice. This effectively pastes the Dreamweaver API call to your text editor. The code can be copied and pasted into an extension as if you went into an extension file and copied the JavaScript directly.

Using Commands from Other Extensions

Commands can take many forms, and one of the most popular uses of a command file is to enhance or expand upon another extension. Some extensions, such as Property Inspectors, are fairly limited in scope and in size, and by linking the inspector to a command file you can accomplish much more in the extension. The ASP.js file in the Inspectors folder of UltraDev does this, as mentioned earlier. The actual inspector only has one button on it, which fires off the command.

The Flash Button object in DW 4 does this as well. When you open the HTML file in the Common folder under Objects, you will be surprised that the file consists of a simple JavaScript include file. Opening up that JavaScript file (Flash Button.js) leads you to the real bull worker of the extension: the Flash Button command, located in the Commands folder. The line that invokes the command is this:

```
retVal = callCommand("Flash Button");
```

Inside the Flash Button.htm and Flash Button.js files in the Commands folder is all of the functionality of the Flash Button object. The interface that you would expect to see in the Objects folder is in the HTML file of the command. This is a case of a Command masquerading as an Object. There are a few good reasons to make a Command take the place of an Object:

▶ Validation is hard to implement in an object, and usually you have to be content with a JavaScript prompt box or no validation at all.

▶ You can define more buttons in a Command and change them on the fly with JavaScript, as just shown.

▶ The command window will stay open until it is explicitly closed with a `window.close()`.

In UltraDev, some of the most complex Server Behaviors are actually commands, such as the Recordset.

Recursion

Recursive techniques are useful in all programming languages, and JavaScript is no exception. Indeed, when dealing with the tree structures of the DOM, sometimes a recursive technique is the best way to tackle a programming problem.

Recursion is simply a method to allow a function to call itself. For a real-world example, suppose you wanted to find some money in a series of successively smaller boxes. Some of them have money in them and some don't, but you will want to look in all of them. You apply your function OpenBox and look inside. Inside that box you find another box. Rather than get out of the box and close it, you reapply the function OpenBox. Inside that box is another. You once again reapply the OpenBox function. You don't stop until all of the boxes are opened. Once you've reached the last box you've exhausted the recursive technique and you can close all the boxes. Regardless of whether you found money in a box, you continued to look inside all of the boxes until they were all opened.

The same thing can be done in programming. For example, suppose you wanted to remove all tags of a specific type from a selection. You could start at the outermost node and then move down the tree until you exhausted each node. You'll do this in the following command extension, called "Strip Tag." The command uses the `findTag()` function of the DOM.js shared file:

```
<html>
<head>
<title>StripTag</title>
<script language="javascript" src="..\Shared\MM\Scripts\CMN\DOM.js"
<script language ="javascript">
```

```
var theTagToRemove = findObject("theTag");
function commandButtons() {
    return new Array("OK", "doCommand()",
                     "Cancel", "window.close()");
    }
function doCommand() {
    // Get all tags and remove
    var getTheTag = findTag(theTagToRemove.value)
    var innerRegion = getTheTag.innerHTML;
    getTheTag.outerHTML = innerRegion;
    if(findTag(theTagToRemove.value)) doCommand();
        window.close()
        }
</script>
</head>
<body>
<form name="theForm" method="post" action="">
<table border="0" cellspacing="2" cellpadding="2">
   <tr>
      <td>
      <p>Tag to remove from document:</p>
      <input type="text" name="theTag" value="">
      </td>
   </tr>
</table>
</form>
</body>
</html>
```

The user can choose the tag to remove, which is assigned to the variable theTagToRemove. The key part of this command is the call inside the doCommand() function to the doCommand() function. This is the recursion in the function. It will call itself over and over until it doesn't find the tag any more, at which point it will get out of the function. Keep in mind that there are many ways to remove tags from a document, and this is one technique.

Adding Head Code

One of the things that you may need to do frequently in an extension is to add code to the head of the document. This is useful when you have to add a function to the script block, or even an inline script. We'll demonstrate this with a command from Massimo Foti: CSS on Platform. This command demonstrates several techniques:

▶ The script that is being inserted into the Web page is executed inline rather than as a function. This makes the extension a perfect candidate for a command. Similar functionality could be accomplished by executing it from the body onLoad() event, but since the code has to execute each time the page loads, it makes sense to include it as an inline script.

▶ The extension searches the document for an existing <script> tag rather than write a new one. Some of the existing commands, such as the Netscape Resize Fix, will write out a new <script> tag regardless of whether or not one already exists.

▶ The command buttons change according to whether or not the script is already in the page. If it is, a Remove button is shown.

▶ The command uses regular expressions to find the script in the page for the various functions.

Building the Extension

First, the extension that is initialized with the <html>, <head>, and <title> tags, along with Massimo's shared file includes:

```
<html>
<head>
<title>CSS on Platform</title>
<script language="javascript"
src="../Shared/Massimocorner/Scripts/DW_dom.js"></script>
<script language="javascript"
src="../Shared/Massimocorner/Scripts/DW_UI.js"></script>
<script language="javascript">
```

Next, the canAcceptCommand() standard API function is defined. This is an optional function and should be called only when necessary to avoid the overhead of the function, since it is called whenever the user chooses the Commands menu. One of the reasons for calling this command is the fact that a command could fail on the Macintosh when the user has no window open (this is impossible to do on the PC).

```
function canAcceptCommand(){
return ((dw.getFocus() == 'document' ||
```

```
          dw.getFocus(true) == 'html' || dw.getFocus() == 'textView'));
}
```

Next, the `commandButtons()` function is declared. If the document already contains the script (verified in the `hasScript()` function) the Add Script, Remove Script, and Cancel buttons are shown. If the `hasScript()` function returns false, only the Add Script and Cancel buttons are shown:

```
function commandButtons(){
    var retArr;
    if(hasScript()){
      retArr = new Array("Add Script", "addScript()",
                         "Remove Script", "removeScript()",
                         "Cancel","window.close()");
    } else {
        retArr = new Array("Add Script","addScript()",
                           "Cancel","window.close()");
    }
    return retArr;
}
```

The `addScript()` function is declared next, which is fired off by the Add Script button in the command interface. This function first grabs the user-defined attributes.

```
function addScript(){
    var macField,winField,Myscript,theDOM,theScriptNodes,theHeadNode;
    //make sure both form fields are filled out
    macField = checkEmpty("MAC");
    winField = checkEmpty("WIN");
```

Next, the string that is to be inserted in the document is built up, piece by piece. This is similar to what was done with Objects in Chapter 2.

```
//If data are valid
if(macField && winField){
//Define the script to insert
Myscript = "";
Myscript += "//tmtC_cssOnPlatform\r";
Myscript += "tmt_css_Mac = \"" + findObject("MAC").value + "\";\r";
Myscript += "tmt_css_Win = \"" + findObject("WIN").value + "\";\r";
Myscript += "if((navigator.appVersion.indexOf(\"Mac\")!= -1)){\r";
Myscript += "    document.write(\"<link rel='stylesheet' href='\" +
```

```
                    tmt_css_Mac + \"' type='text/css'>\");\r";
Myscript += "}\r";
Myscript += "else{\r";
Myscript += "   document.write(\"<link rel='stylesheet' href='\" +
                    tmt_css_Win + \"' type='text/css'>\");\r";
Myscript += "}//tmtC_cssOnPlatformEnd";
```

Now that you have the code to be inserted into the document, you have to figure out whether the document already has a script tag or not. This is done with the `hasScript()` function. Notice that Massimo uses plain English function definitions so that the code is readable by anyone. If the document already contains the script, the regular expression that begins with tmtC_cssOnPlatform and ends with tmtC_cssOnPlatformEnd will allow you to replace the section of code with the new code contained in the Myscript variable:

```
//Get the DOM and do the job
theDOM = dw.getDocumentDOM();
theScriptNodes = theDOM.getElementsByTagName("SCRIPT");
//Check if the is already there
theHeadNode = theDOM.getElementsByTagName("HEAD");
//If the script is already there, just replace it
if(hasScript()){
    var oldHead,pattern,newHead;
    oldHead = theHeadNode.item(0).innerHTML;
    pattern =
    /\/\/tmtC_cssOnPlatform[a-zA-Z0-9]*[^$]*tmtC_cssOnPlatformEnd/g;
    //Replace the old script with the new one
    newHead = oldHead.replace(pattern, Myscript);
    //Put the new code in the head of the doc
    theHeadNode[0].innerHTML = newHead;
    }
```

If the script isn't already in the document, look for a set of `<script>` tags. The script tag has to be one that isn't a reference to an external js file (if it has the src attribute, then you should reject the set of script tags and move to the next). If the `<script>` tags exist, add your inline script after the existing script, before the closing tag. If no script tags exist in the document, add a set around the code contained in the Myscript variable and add it to the `<head>` tag:

```
//The script is not there, do our job
 else{
```

```
    var jsScripts,goodScripts;
    //Filter the script tags to find only the one without SRC
    jsScripts = matchNoAttribute(theScriptNodes,"SRC");
    //Get only the Javascript tags
    goodScripts = matchAttributeValue(jsScripts,"language","javascript");
    //If there is any
    if(goodScripts.length>0){
        goodScripts[0].innerHTML = goodScripts[0].innerHTML + Myscript;
        }
    else{
        //Create the new script tag and put the script inside
        theHeadNode[0].innerHTML = theHeadNode[0].innerHTML +
        "<script language=\"javascript\">\r" + Myscript + "\r</s" +
        "cript>";
        }
    }
    window.close();
    }
}
```

The `removeScript()` function is declared next. This function will effectively remove the CSS on Platform command from the current document by using the same regular expression pattern that was used in the previous function. The comments serve as a guide to match the code in the document. This technique is used extensively by extension writers, and it even forms the basis of the way that Server Behaviors are implemented in UltraDev. Macromedia uses the MM_ prefix in its code. Most extension writers have their own prefix patterns that identify their code in a user's document; it makes it much easier to find the code when you need to.

```
function removeScript(){
var pattern,theDOM,theHeadInHTML;
pattern =
   /\/\/tmtC_cssOnPlatform[_a-zA-Z0-9\-]*[^$]*tmtC_cssOnPlatformEnd/g;
//Get the DOM and do the job
theDOM = dw.getDocumentDOM();
//Take the HTML out of the head and clean it
newHeadInHTML =
theDOM.getElementsByTagName("HEAD")[0].innerHTML.replace(pattern,"");
theDOM.getElementsByTagName("HEAD")[0].innerHTML = newHeadInHTML;
cleanEmptyScripts(theDOM);
window.close();
}
```

Next is the hasScript() function, which will perform a simple regular expression *test* method to see if the tmtC_cssOnPlatform script is contained on the page—the test is performed only on the innerHTML of the <head> tag. This is where the script would be if it were in the document, so there is no point testing the document any further.

```
function hasScript(){
  var pattern = /tmtC_cssOnPlatform/;
return
pattern.test(dw.getDocumentDOM().getElementsByTagName("HEAD")[0].innerHTML);
}
```

The User Interface

The next part of the extension is the user interface functionality. Typically in this part of the extension you have to load the user interface with values from the document if the extension already exists in the document. If it doesn't, the function will simply leave the text fields blank. Once again, a regular expression is used to find the script in the document and extract the values for the .css files for both platform types (Windows and Mac):

```
// ---------- UI Functions  ---------
function populateUI(){
var thePageDom,oldHead;
thePageDom = dw.getDocumentDOM("document");
//If the code in inside the doc, populate the form
if(hasScript()){
   var macPattern,winPattern,macValue,winValue;
   //Get the head of the doc
   oldHead = thePageDom.getElementsByTagName("HEAD")[0].innerHTML;
   //Match the Mac value
   macPattern = /tmt_css_Mac = "[_a-zA-Z0-9\-]*\.css";/;
   macValue = oldHead.match(macPattern);
   //Match the Win value
   winPattern = /tmt_css_Win = "[_a-zA-Z0-9\-]*\.css";/;
   winValue = oldHead.match(winPattern);
   //If we got some value, populate the text fields
   if(macValue){
      findObject("MAC").value =
          macValue[0].match(/[_a-zA-Z0-9\-]*\.css/);
   }
   if(winValue){
      findObject("WIN").value =
```

```
                winValue[0].match(/[_a-zA-Z0-9\-]*\.css/);
        }
    }
}
```

Next is the `initializeUI()` function, which is typical for an extension that has a user interface. The function checks for the script first, and if it finds it, calls the `populateUI()` function and puts the appropriate .css filenames into the textfields. Next, it sets the focus to the first textfield in the interface: NN.

```
function initializeUI(){
    if(hasScript()){
    populateUI();
    }
    //Set focus on textbox
    findObject("MAC").focus();
    //Set insertion point into textbox
    findObject("MAC").select();
}
```

That does it for the head functions, so close up the script and head tags and define a CSS style for the text fields for the user interface. This is done to keep the style consistent across platforms, since you can define pixels and not worry about font sizes:

```
</script>
<style type="text/css">
.shortTextField {  width: 135px}
</style>
</head>
```

Next is the user interface, which is abbreviated from the original multitabbed interface. Massimo's multitabbed interfaces have become something of a standard in Dreamweaver extensibility, and the reader is advised to look at some of the available extensions for the techniques used. We've stripped it down to the bare essentials here because of space constraints. The interface consists of two text fields, each with its own browse button to browse for a .css file:

```
<body onload="initializeUI()">
  <form>
      <table>
          <tr>
              <td colspan="2">Insert a script inside the head of your page
that loads an external CSS file depending on platform</td>
          </tr>
```

```
      <tr>
        <td nowrap valign="baseline">Mac:</td>
        <td nowrap>
          <input type="text" name="MAC" class="shortTextField">
          <input type="submit" name="MAC_BUTTON" value="Browse"
                      onClick="browseFile('MAC')">
        </td>
      </tr>
      <tr>
        <td nowrap valign="baseline">Win:</td>
        <td nowrap>
          <input type="text" name="WIN" class="shortTextField">
          <input type="submit" name="WIN_BUTTON" value="Browse"
                      onClick="browseFile('WIN')">
        </td>
      </tr>
    </table>
  </form>
</body>
</html>
```

Menu Commands

A menu command is nothing more than a command that is executed from a menu. The menu command is generally stored in the Configuration | Menus folder and can be placed directly in that folder or in your own subfolder. Also in this folder is the menus.xml file. The menus.xml file will be examined later in the book, including the methods used for creating your own menu items and menus by creating an MXI file. The menu files can also be edited by hand using Notepad, BBEdit, or your text editor of choice. It should be noted that the menus.xml file is not true XML. XML editors such as XML Spy, XMetaL, or XML Notepad will flag it as invalid XML.

The menu command API is documented in the Extending Dreamweaver 4 document that comes with Dreamweaver and UltraDev. The menu command API has a few extra functions that are not contained in the command API that make working with the menus a little easier. In addition to the standard command API function calls, `canAcceptCommand()`, `commandButtons()`, `receiveArguments()`, and `windowDimensions()`, there are a few new calls that deal solely with the menu command extension.

`getDynamicContent()` is a function that is called if the `<menuitem>` tag contains a *dynamic* attribute. This attribute allows you to build dynamic menus based on criteria established by the user, the extension, the selection, site preferences, or any number of other criteria. This makes it very easy to customize the menu system on-the-fly from within your extension. We'll demonstrate this technique with a new menu command called Open With, which does just what it describes—it allows the user to open the current document in whatever program she wants to from a list that is user-defined as well.

Creating the Set Text Editor Prefs Command

This command exists solely to create a preference file for the user. The file is a standard Dreamweaver design note file (with an .mno file extension). These files are XML files that can be used by the extension developer to store various settings that might be needed. Each extension can have its own design note file to store whatever information you need about the extension. In this case, the extension is going to store the user's preferred editors. These can be text editors, other Web development programs like Homesite or CF Studio, or utility programs like WinZip—in short, any program that you might need to use in conjunction with Dreamweaver or UltraDev.

The interface for the Set Text Editor Prefs command will be a familiar style of interface to the Dreamweaver user. Whenever possible, it's wise to stick to the standard styles of interface that Dreamweaver users come to expect. This one will feature a list box with a plus and minus button for adding and removing items from the box, as shown in Figure 3-4.

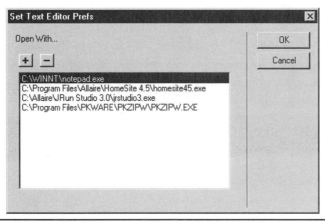

Figure 3-4   *The interface for the Set Text Editor Prefs command*

Start by creating the shell for the extension, leaving a space to insert your JavaScript functions:

```
<!-- MENU-LOCATION=NONE -->
<html>
<head>
<script
src="../Shared/MM/Scripts/Class/ListControlClass.js"></script>
<script language="javascript">
var LIST_FILES = new ListControl("editorList");
//the JavaScript functions will go here!

</script>
<title>Set Text Editor Prefs</title>
</head>
<body onLoad="initializeUI()">
<form>
<table width="100%" border="0" cellspacing="0" cellpadding="0">
   <tr>
      <td valign="baseline" nowrap> Open With... <br>
      </td>
   </tr>
   <tr>
      <td valign="top">
        <input type="image" src="../shared/MM/images/btnAdd.gif"
         name="btnIncludeFile" onClick="addFilename();">
        <input type="image" src="../shared/MM/images/btnDel.gif"
         name="btnExcludeFile" onClick="removeSelectedFilenames();"
      </td>
    <tr>
      <td>
         <select name="editorList" style="width:300px" size="12">
         </select><br>
      </td>
        </tr>
</table>
</form>
</body>
</html>
```

It's a relatively simple interface, with a list box and two image buttons, which are taken from the MM shared image file. If you want to get fancy, you can add the mouse-down images, which are located in the same directory. Examples of mouseDown functionality can be found in existing Dreamweaver extensions. The image buttons are tied to the functions that allow you to add or remove filenames from the list box.

Next, insert the standard API calls and extension initialization that is necessary for the command:

```
function commandButtons() { // set up the OK and Cancel buttons
   var retArr;
   retArr = new Array("OK","saveSettings()",
                    "Cancel","window.close()");
   return retArr;
   }
function initializeUI() { // initialize a listbox using the
                      // ListControlClass from the MM shared file.
   LIST_FILES  = new ListControl("editorList");
   theList = getArrayPreferences('FileList');
   LIST_FILES.setAll(theList,theList);
   }
```

The `commandButtons()` API function creates two buttons, OK and Cancel. The `initializeUI()` function instantiates an instance of ListControlClass. If you haven't used this class yet, it's located in the Configuration | Shared | MM | Scripts | Classes folder and is well documented within the file itself. Using this class makes it much easier to work with list boxes within Dreamweaver.

The Design Notes Functions

The list box is named LIST_FILES and will contain the list of filenames that will be the user-defined program list. The list comes from the design notes, which need to be set up in the following functions:

```
function saveArrayPreferences(theSetting,theArray) {
    if (typeof MMNotes == 'undefined') {return;}
    // Check for MMNotes extension.
    var metaFile, theString;
    theString = theArray.join();//array into a comma-separated list
    metaFile = MMNotes.open(document.URL, true);
    if (metaFile) {
        //Set the value of the key
        MMNotes.set(metaFile,theSetting,theString);
        }
    MMNotes.close(metaFile);
    }
function getArrayPreferences(theSetting){
    if (typeof MMNotes == 'undefined') {return null;}
```

```
     // Check for MMNotes extension.
     var theString, metaFile;
     var theArray = new Array();
     metaFile = MMNotes.open(document.URL, true);
     if (metaFile) {
         //Get the value of the key
         settingValue = MMNotes.get(metaFile,theSetting);
         //If we have any saved setting
         if(settingValue){
             theArray = settingValue.split(',');
         }
     }
MMNotes.close(metaFile);
return theArray;
}
```

The design notes functions are based on a library of design note functions in DW_settings.js by Massimo Foti and are scaled down versions of those functions. That library is useful for saving preferences from any extension that saves the user preferences of form fields. These two functions are also generic and can be saved in a shared library for use by any command. The `saveArrayPreferences()` function will save an array as a comma-separated list in a name/value pair inside the design notes. The `getArrayPreferences()` function will get the csv list back from the design notes and place it into an array.

Updating the User Interface

Next, the functions take care of updating the user interface when the user clicks the plus or minus button. The `removeSelectedFilenames()` function uses the del() method of the ListControlClass, which simply removes the selected item from the list. The `addFilename()` function uses the add method of the class after it has retrieved a filename from the `getFullFilePath()` function:

```
function removeSelectedFilenames() {
    var theList = document.forms[0].editorList;
    for (var i=0; i<theList.options.length;i++) {
        if(theList.options[i].selected) LIST_FILES.del();
        }
    }
function addFilename() {
    var newEditor = getFullFilePath();
```

```
        if(newEditor != null && newEditor != "")
            LIST_FILES.add(newEditor); //add a new listbox entry
}
function getFullFilePath() {
        var thePath = getFullPath(dw.browseForFileURL('select',
          'Choose an additional doc editor',true));
        thePath = thePath.replace(/file:\/\/\/([^\|]*)\|/,"$1:");
        thePath = thePath.replace(/\//g,'\\') ;
        return thePath;
        }
```

Lastly, when the user clicks OK, the `saveSettings()` function is fired off, which will save the list into the design notes as just described:

```
function saveSettings() {
        saveArrayPreferences('FileList',LIST_FILES.get('all'));
        window.close();
        }
```

You may have noticed that the command has a `<!-- MENU-LOCATION=NONE -->` tag right at the top of the file. This command is called directly from a custom menu item, so it shouldn't appear on the menu in another location. The menu will be addressed next.

Creating the Menu Items

For now, you can edit the menus.xml file by hand and add these lines right after the last `<menuitem>` tag in the DWMenu_Commands menu but before the closing `</menu>` tag for that particular menu. The lines will look like this:

```
<menu name="Open With..." id="TFM_DWMenu_Commands_OpenWith">
  <menuitem dynamic name="(none)" arguments="'(none)'"
    enabled="true" file="Menus/Open With.htm"
    id="TFM_DWContext_Text_OpenWithx" />
<separator />
    <menuitem name="Change Editor Prefs..." enabled="true"
      command="dw.runCommand('Set Text Editor Prefs')"
      id="TFM_DWMenu_Commands_OpenWithPref" />
</menu>
```

The `<menu>` tag sets up a menu named Open With. This will be the menu item that you can choose from the Commands menu that will cause the submenu to open up. The submenu will be dynamic since the dynamic attribute is used in the `<menuitem>` tag. The current menu item is the dummy item that will only be seen if there are no dynamic menu items, such as when you first install the extension. The file attribute points to the Menus/Open With.htm file, which will be the main command file for this extension.

The next `<menuitem>` tag refers to the Set Text Editor Prefs command, which was just built. When the user chooses this menu item, the command is run with the `dw.runCommand()` API call.

The Open With Command

The last part of the operation is to build the actual menu command—Open With. Start by creating the shell of the user interface:

```
<html>
<head>
<title>Open With...</title>
<script language="javascript">
var theFile; // variable that will hold a filename
var menuItems = new Array(); // array for the menuitem list
var theList = new Array();  // array for the list of programs
// JavaScript functions go here!
</script>
</head>
<body onLoad="openWith()">
</body>
</html>
```

Three variables are defined as globals because they have to be accessed from various parts of the extension. The `<body>` tag `onLoad` event calls the main function for the extension—`openWith()`. Before getting to that function, however, there are two menu command API functions that will be called by Dreamweaver:

```
// *************** Commands API ***************
function getDynamicContent() {
  var stringArray = new Array();
  getTextEditorList();
  for(var i=0; i<theList.length; i++) {
    menuItems[i] = theList[i] + " ;id='" +
        "TFM_DWMenu_Commands_OpenWith" + i + "'";
    }
   return menuItems;
```

```
}
function receiveArguments() {
   theFile = arguments[0];
}
```

getDynamicContent() is called whenever a user chooses a menu and there
is a dynamic attribute in the menu item. In this function, the list of user-defined text
editors is retrieved from the getTextEditorList() function. The dynamic
menu is then built as an array (as specified in the Dreamweaver API documents).
Dreamweaver expects an array to be returned from the function and will create the
menu based on that array. The receiveArguments() function is called when
the user chooses a menu item in that menu. The argument returned in this case is
an ID attribute for the menu item.

The getTextEditorList() function is similar to the
getArrayPreferences() function that was created for the Get Text Editor
Prefs command. It is designed to retrieve the information from the design note that
was written in the Get Text Editor Prefs command:

```
function getTextEditorList() {
    if (typeof MMNotes == 'undefined') {return;}
  // Check for MMNotes extension.
      var theSettings,metaFile;
      metaFile = MMNotes.open(dw.getConfigurationPath() +
        "/Commands/Set Text Editor Prefs.htm", true);
      if (metaFile) {
          var settingValue;
          //Get the value of the key
          settingValue = MMNotes.get(metaFile,'FileList');
          //If we have any saved setting
          if(settingValue){
              theList = settingValue.split(',');
          }
      }
      MMNotes.close(metaFile);
  }
```

This is a custom version of the original function. Since the function has to retrieve
the preferences from a *different* command, you can't use the generic function; you
have to hard-code the original command name (/Commands/Set Text Editor Prefs.htm)
in the function.

Next, the main `openWith()` function is declared, which will do the work of opening the current document in the program that the user chooses from the dynamic menu:

```
function openWith() {
if(theFile == "(none)")return; //no menu items defined
// at this point theFile contains the menu item chosen by the user
var theEditor, theEditor;
theEditorPath =
theList[theFile.replace(/TFM_DWMenu_Commands_OpenWith(\d+)/,'$1')]
theEditor = theEditorPath.slice(theEditorPath.lastIndexOf('\\')+1);
    var MSG_Err_FileNotSaved =
        "This file must be saved prior to opening with ";
    var MSG_Err_FileNotSaved2 = "\n\nDo you want to save it now?";
    if (dreamweaver.getDocumentPath("document") == "" ) {
      if (confirm(MSG_Err_FileNotSaved + theEditor +
        MSG_Err_FileNotSaved2) &&
dw.canSaveDocument(dreamweaver.getDocumentDOM('document'))) {
      dw.saveDocument(dreamweaver.getDocumentDOM('document'));
      }
    if ( dreamweaver.getDocumentPath( "document" ) == "" ) return;
}
dreamweaver.openWithApp(dreamweaver.getDocumentPath("document"),
  theEditorPath);
  theList = null;
  menuItems = null;
  window.close();
  return;
}
```

This function first checks to see whether or not the document has already been saved. If it hasn't, a JavaScript *confirm* box pops up and the user must choose OK to save the file or Cancel. If the user chooses Cancel, the function fails and exits.

After building the two command files and making the menu changes, the command is ready for use and can be accessed from the Commands menu. After adding a few items to the menu, it might look like Figure 3-5, which shows four different menu items that are stored in the design notes for the command.

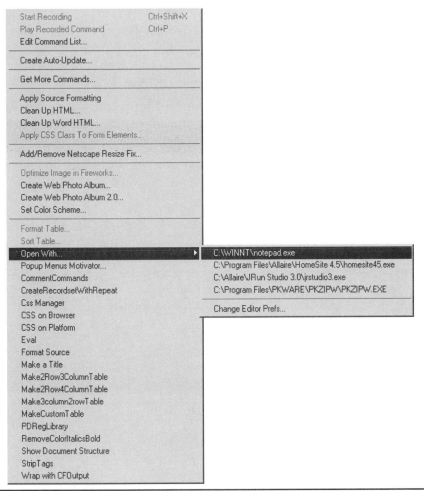

Figure 3-5   *Accessing the new command from the Commands menu shows the dynamic menu items*

What to Take Away from this Chapter

Commands are probably the most versatile extensions to work with as well as the hardest to describe. If you have to describe what commands do, the answer would have to be *anything*. Commands can be called from anywhere and are only limited by the extension developer's imagination.

Exercises

1. Change the Comment commands so that they work with JavaScript comments. Hint: you can't use the *comment* node type anymore.

2. Build a command that finds a possible link in the document using regular expressions and adds an `<a href>` tag around the text. Hint: you have to make sure the text doesn't have a link around it already.

3. Adapt the CSS on Platform extension so that it can become a CSS on Browser command instead.

Property Inspectors and Floaters

IN THIS CHAPTER:

The main functional extensions of Dreamweaver are the Objects, Behaviors, and Commands, but there are some other extensions that the extensionologist should be familiar with—Floaters and Property Inspectors. Floaters can add functionality to the Dreamweaver environment and can be docked with the standard Dreamweaver palettes. Property Inspectors typically don't add to the functionality of the program but offer a common interface to the properties of the currently selected object or code.

Property Inspectors

Inspectors, or Property Inspectors as they are also known, are the Floaters that display the properties of an object or behavior that is selected in the design environment. Many of the built-in Inspectors are written in C and are intrinsic to the functionality of Dreamweaver, such as the Table Inspector. Inspectors can also be written in JavaScript to override the standard Property Inspectors, and you can write custom Inspectors for your custom Object, Data Source, Behavior, Server Behavior, or custom tag. Like Translators, they don't usually exist as units by themselves but rather complement an existing extension by providing a user interface for editing the attributes of a selected extension or tag. Property Inspectors can also be written to allow the user to be able to edit the attributes of any tag, such as the body tag.

CAUTION

A Property Inspector is the only Floater that isn't dockable. Also, its size is fixed, unlike the other Floaters.

The Interface of a Property Inspector

The Inspector interface is built just like the interfaces for other extensions, such as Objects and Commands. The interface, however, must conform to certain Macromedia standards as far as size and placement. The Property Inspectors appear when you choose Window | Properties. You'll notice that the narrow box that appears doesn't have a lot of room for attributes. Most Property Inspectors call commands from the various buttons that appear on the Inspector. In Figure 4-1, which depicts a standard ASP Inspector, you'll notice that the entire Inspector consists of just one button: Edit. By clicking the button, a code window is invoked by the EditContent command. Other Inspectors can be more complicated and contain many attributes and commands, as in the Table Inspector (see Figure 4-2).

Figure 4-1   *The standard ASP Property Inspector has just one button*

Since the real estate of the Property Inspector box is so scarce, many Inspectors are written using Layers instead of Tables. This allows for more precise placement of your attribute fields within the confines of the Inspector. The layers themselves generally contain tables to allow for even more precise placement.

The interface can be designed in the Dreamweaver environment. Use the Layer Object from the Common Objects tab to precisely place your layers in the interface, and then place your text and form elements in smaller tables within the layers. The Layer Floater can then be used to select individual layers as you are working with the extension.

TIP

Turning off invisible elements from the View | Visual Aids menu can make life easier when you are building your Property Inspector interface.

The Property Inspector has two states, expanded and collapsed. The fully expanded Inspector measures 87 pixels high by 482 pixels wide. You collapse a Property Inspector by clicking on the little arrow in the lower right corner of the Inspector. Generally, the main attributes are in the top half of the Inspector and other attributes are in the lower half.

The Property Inspector works a little differently than other extensions in that there is no OK button with which to save your changes. When you make a change in the Property Inspector, it's immediate, so you have to code it accordingly. The interface

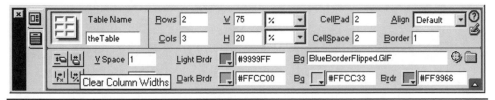

Figure 4-2   *The Table Inspector is overflowing with attributes and buttons*

code is described in the next paragraph. Pay particular attention to the function calls on the onBlur and onChange events of the form objects. Since we are dealing with an Inspector, the changes in the document occur on-the-fly as you are entering information into the Inspector. Also, notice the layers used.

After placing the form elements in the Dreamweaver environment inside of Layers, there is a little bit of code manipulation involved to get the elements to appear properly. The best way to do this is by trial and error using the built-in Dreamweaver grid or by using a *tracing image*. Tracing images come in handy for building Web sites but are also useful for laying out your extension interfaces. A tracing image can be chosen by going to the View menu and the Tracing Image | Load command. The Tracing Image interface is shown in Figure 4-3. This can be an image of an existing Inspector, which can be used as a model for your own Inspector, or it can be a custom grid image. Simply save the image as a JPEG at the size of 482×87 pixels. After loading in the image, you need to set the X and Y positions by going to the Tracing Image | Adjust Position menu item and setting the position to X-0 and Y-0. Set the transparency to about 20–30%. Then you can use it

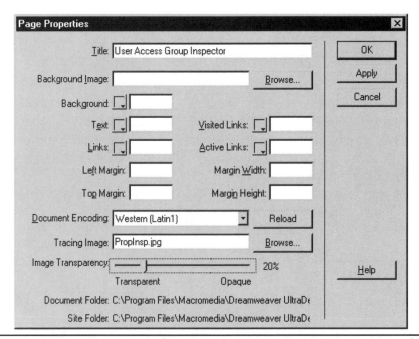

Figure 4-3   *The Tracing Image interface; note that you can set the transparency of the image (20–30% is usually good)*

as a guide for positioning your layers and elements. Figure 4-4 shows an Inspector being designed over a tracing image.

TIP

Tracing images are great time savers when you have to design a Web page or an interface that has to conform to certain standards of size or positioning.

Inspecting the Selection

Inspectors generally work by examining a selection and determining the attributes of the selected object, tag, or script block. They can also examine the attributes of an area that the cursor is within. Inspectors are constantly changing within the confines

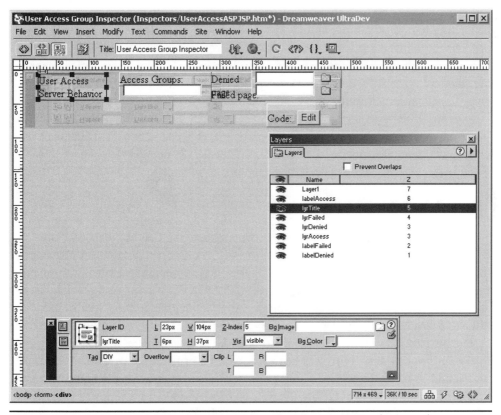

Figure 4-4 *An Inspector being designed over a "tracing image," a feature of Dreamweaver that resides in the View menu*

of Dreamweaver. As the user moves the cursor on the page or inserts new objects or code, Dreamweaver is constantly searching for an Inspector to display. If you leave the Property Inspector closed, Dreamweaver can run a little faster because it's not inspecting your selection each time you make a change in the page.

There are two mandatory functions in the Property Inspector—`inspectSelection()` and `canInspectSelection()`. In addition, you can specify a `displayHelp()` function in your Inspector, as in all extensions, and the help dialog that you choose will be displayed when the user clicks the little question mark in the top right corner of the Inspector. This question mark will only appear when the `displayHelp()` function is declared. The help can be a simple alert box, an HTML page in your shared folder, or a link to a Web page.

Form Inspector

Massimo Foti has created some of the most popular Dreamweaver extensions. What better way to describe how to build an Inspector than to go through the code of one of Massimo's Inspector extensions? We'll dissect the Form Inspector that Massimo wrote to take the place of the standard Form Inspector. Massimo built this because the standard Form Inspector was missing functionality of the standard form attribute *enctype* and target attributes of the `<form>` tag.

The top of the Inspector contains a comment string as the very first line. All Inspectors must have this string or they won't work. This is the line that Dreamweaver will search for to determine which Inspector to display. It contains the main attributes of the Inspector file. Put this line at the beginning of the file:

```
<!-- tag:FORM,priority:4,selection:within,hline -->
```

The string starts with the *tag* attribute, which is the tag that the Inspector is to be used for. In this case, we're using the Inspector for `<form>` tags. An Inspector that is for server-side code in UltraDev (that is, code contained within `<% %>` tags) can use a special class instead of a tag name: *LOCKED*. The other special classes are *COMMENT* and *ASP*, although *ASP* is deprecated in favor of the *LOCKED* class for UltraDev.

The next attribute in the comment string is the *priority*. Since tags can have more than one Property Inspector, you have to specify a priority level, with 1 being the lowest and 10 being the highest. Dreamweaver always begins with the highest priority level item and moves down from there. You can have a whole series of Inspectors for any given tag and have different priority levels for each, depending on the set of parameters you define in the `canInspectSelection()` function, which we'll describe later. It's best to keep the priority levels lower (in the 4–5 range).

TIP

The built-in Property Inspectors have a priority level that is lower than 1; so if you use a value of 1, you can override the use of a standard Dreamweaver Inspector.

Next is the *selection* attribute. This can be set to either *exact* or *within*, depending on whether the selection can be within the tag or must be exactly contained in the tag. The *hline* and *vline* attributes refer to the actual Inspector interface. In the standard ASP Inspector shown in Figure 4-2, there is a horizontal line going through the center of the interface. This is the *hline* attribute. If you don't specify it, the line won't be there. The *vline* attribute generally divides the title of the Inspector from the properties. You can see this in Figure 4-2 to the left of the Table Name attribute separating it from the other properties. By clicking the little arrow at the bottom right corner of the Inspector you can collapse the Inspector up to the *hline*. Generally, you put the main properties in the top half of the Inspector, and any secondary properties in the lower half.

Next, the HTML interface is created. We'll break it up into pieces to better understand it. First, here are the opening tags and script declarations:

```
<html>
<head>
<title>Form Property Inspector</title>
<!--inspector "Form"
Version: 1.2
Copyright © 2001 Massimocorner.com
Developed 2001 Massimo Foti (massimo@massimocorner.com)
-->
<script language="JavaScript"
src="../Shared/Massimocorner/Scripts/DW_UI.js"></script>
<script language="JavaScript">
//functions go here!
</script>
```

Next, three styles are set up for the text fields. These are set to exact pixel values so that the compatibility across platforms is improved. In this Inspector we have three different sized text fields: `shortTextField`, `longTextField`, and `veryLongTextField`. The descriptive names of the style classes let you know exactly what they are used for:

```
<style type="text/css">
<!--
.shortTextField {
    width: 80px;
```

```
}
.longTextField {
    width: 110px;
}
.veryLongTextField {
    width: 220px;
}
-->
</style>
</head>
```

Next, the body of the Inspector is coded. The first `<span>` tag houses the image that serves as the icon for the Inspector in the upper left corner, and is in fact the same icon used by the standard Form Inspector that is built into Dreamweaver.

```
<body>
<span id="image" style="position:absolute; width:23px; height:17px;
z-index:1; left: 3px; top: 2px">
<img src="../Shared/Massimocorner/Images/icon_form.gif"
width="36" height="36">
</span>
```

Next, the main interface of the Inspector is written. Notice that the *id* properties of the `<span>` tags describe what will be housed inside of them. The top half of the Inspector has the main properties of the `<form>` tag that it is inspecting, which are the forms *name* and the *action*.

```
<form name="theForm">
<span id="mainProperties" style="position:absolute;
 z-index:1; left: 48px; top: 5px">
<table border="0" cellspacing="0" cellpadding="0">
   <tr>
     <td nowrap valign="baseline">Name</td>
     <td nowrap>
       <input type="text" name="THE_NAME"
        class="longTextField" onBlur="setAttributes()">
        </td>
     <td> </td>
     <td> </td>
     <td valign="baseline">Action</td>
     <td> </td>
     <td nowrap valign="baseline">
```

```
      <input type="text" name="THE_ACTION"
        class="veryLongTextField" onBlur="setAttributes()">
    </td>
    <td> </td>
    <td nowrap valign="baseline">
      <input type="image" border="0" name="imageField"
        src="../Shared/Massimocorner/Images/icon_folder.gif"
        width="15" height="13"
        onClick="browseFile('THE_ACTION');setAttributes()">
    </td>
    <td> </td>
  </tr>
</table>
</span>
```

The lower half of the Inspector contains the *target, method,* and *enctype* properties of the <form> tag, which are defined as drop-down lists.

```
<span id="moreProperties" style="position:absolute;
 z-index:1; left: 48px; top: 54px">
<table border="0" cellspacing="0" cellpadding="0">
   <tr>
     <td nowrap valign="baseline">Target</td>
     <td nowrap>
       <select name="THE_TARGET" class="shortTextField"
        onChange="setAttributes()">
         <option></option>
       </select>
     </td>
     <td> </td>
     <td> </td>
     <td nowrap>Enctype</td>
     <td> </td>
     <td>
       <select name="THE_ENC" class="longTextField"
        onChange="setAttributes()">
         <option>Default</option>
         <option>multipart/form-data</option>
         <option>text/plain</option>
       </select>
     </td>
     <td> </td>
```

```
   <td>Method:</td>
   <td>
    <select name="THE_METHOD" class="shortTextField"
     onChange="setAttributes()">
      <option>Default</option>
      <option>GET</option>
      <option>POST</option>
    </select></td>
  </tr>
</table>
</span>
</form>
</body>
</html>
```

The most difficult part of building the Inspector file is usually the construction of the interface. With that out of the way, you can now focus on the functionality by defining some of the API calls and other helper functions that the Inspector will need.

The canInspectSelection Function

This function does the job of telling Dreamweaver whether the current selection is a valid candidate to display the Inspector. The function can do whatever is required to determine this. In this case, the only requirement is that the currently selected object is a <form> tag, so a helper function, getSelectedObj(), is declared and is then called from the canInspectSelection() function:

```
//Returns the selected object
function getSelectedObj(){
    var selArr=dreamweaver.getSelection();

    return dreamweaver.offsetsToNode(selArr[0],selArr[1]);
}
function canInspectSelection(){
    var theObj = getSelectedObj();
    return (theObj.tagName == "FORM");
}
```

The getSelectedObject() function is actually a standard Dreamweaver shared function that can be found in the shared folder. One thing you should consider when developing extensions is including the actual shared functions used by your extension in your own shared file or in the extension itself. The benefit is not immediately apparent, but after you've had an extension stop working because a shared function that you once used is no longer located in the same place, you'll appreciate this. A well-known case is the UltraDev Shopping Cart extension in which the Save Cart behavior stopped working after a shared file location changed from UltraDev 1 to UltraDev 4. Although most of the documented shared functions are not likely to go anywhere, you can never be sure—it's better to be safe than sorry.

CAUTION

One thing to keep in mind if you put the shared functions in your own file, however, is that if a function changes in the future, such as when `MM_findObj()` changed from version 4 to version 4.01, your code will have to be updated.

The inspectSelection Function

The `inspectSelection()` function is called after `canInspectSelection()` returns a "true" to UltraDev. What this function has to do is to take the selection apart and separate the static code from the user-defined attributes and then display the attributes in the user interface. Inspectors do it on-the-fly and don't have to wait for the user to hit OK. For an HTML tag, the `inspectSelection()` function is relatively easy. There is a standard Dreamweaver API function `getAttribute()` that will return an attribute of a tag. Here is the `inspectSelection()` function:

```
function inspectSelection(){
    //Store the selected object in a var
    var theFormObj = getSelectedObj();
    if (theFormObj.getAttribute("action")){
        findObject("THE_ACTION").value =
            theFormObj.getAttribute("action");

    }

    else{

        findObject("THE_ACTION").value= "";
    }

    if (theFormObj.getAttribute("name")){

        findObject("THE_NAME").value =
            theFormObj.getAttribute("name");
    }
    else{
```

```
        findObject("THE_NAME").value = "";
    }
    //Handle enctype attribute
    var encValue,encSelect;
    var encArray = new Array("","multipart/form-data","text/plain");
    encSelect = findObject("THE_ENC");
    encValue = theFormObj.getAttribute("enctype");
    if(encValue){
        for(var i=0; i<encSelect.options.length; i++){
            if(encSelect.options[i].text.toLowerCase() ==
                encValue.toLowerCase()){
                encSelect.options[i].selected = true;
                break;
            }
        }
    }
    else{

        encSelect.selectedIndex = 0;
    }
    //Handle method attribute
    var methodValue,methodSelect;
    methodSelect = findObject("THE_METHOD");
    methodValue = theFormObj.getAttribute("method");
    if(methodValue){
        for(var i=0; i<methodSelect.options.length; i++){
            if(methodSelect.options[i].text.toLowerCase() ==
                methodValue.toLowerCase()){
                methodSelect.options[i].selected = true;
                break;
            }
        }
    }
    else{
        methodSelect.selectedIndex = 0;
    }
//Now the target
    var targetArray,docFrames,targetMenu,targetValue;
    targetArray = new Array("","_blank","_parent","_self","_top");
    docFrames = dw.getDocumentDOM().getFrameNames();
    if(docFrames){
        targetArray = targetArray.concat(docFrames);
    }
```

```
    populateSelect("THE_TARGET",targetArray);
    targetMenu = findObject("THE_TARGET");
    targetValue = theFormObj.getAttribute("target");
    if(targetValue){
        for(var i=0; i<targetMenu.options.length; i++){
            if(targetMenu.options[i].text.toLowerCase() ==
                targetValue.toLowerCase()){
                targetMenu.options[i].selected = true;
                break;
            }
        }
    }
    else{
        targetMenu.selectedIndex = 0;
    }
}
```

Other Custom Support Functions

The function that does the work of updating the code in the document is
setAttributes(), the custom code-insertion routine for this Inspector.
The function is as follows:

```
function setAttributes(){
    //Store the selected object in a var
    var theFormObj = getSelectedObj();
    if (findObject("THE_NAME").value){
        theFormObj.setAttribute("name",findObject("THE_NAME").value);
    }
    else{
        theFormObj.removeAttribute("name");
    }
    if (findObject("THE_ACTION").value){

theFormObj.setAttribute("action",findObject("THE_ACTION").value);
    }
    else{
        theFormObj.removeAttribute("THE_ACTION");
    }
    //Handle enctype attribute
    var whichEnc,encSelect;
    var encArray = new Array("","multipart/form-data","text/plain");
    encSelect = findObject("THE_ENC");
```

```
for(var h=0; h<encSelect.options.length; h++){
    if (encSelect.options[h].selected){
        whichEnc = encArray[h];
        break;
    }
}
if(whichEnc){
    theFormObj.setAttribute("enctype",whichEnc);
}
else{
    theFormObj.removeAttribute("enctype");
}
//Handle method attribute
var whichMethod,encSelect;
var methodArray = new Array("","GET","POST");
methodSelect = findObject("THE_METHOD");
for(var h=0; h<methodSelect.options.length; h++){
    if (methodSelect.options[h].selected){
        whichMethod = methodArray[h];
        break;
    }
}
if(whichMethod){
    theFormObj.setAttribute("method",whichMethod);
}
else{
    theFormObj.removeAttribute("method");
}
//Now the target
var targetArray,docFrames,targetMenu,whichTarget;
targetArray = new Array("","_blank","_parent","_self","_top");
docFrames = dw.getDocumentDOM().getFrameNames();
if(docFrames){
    targetArray = targetArray.concat(docFrames);
}
targetMenu = findObject("THE_TARGET");
for(var i=0; i<targetMenu.options.length; i++){
    if (targetMenu.options[i].selected){
        whichTarget = targetArray[i];
        break;
    }
}
if(whichTarget){
```

```
        theFormObj.setAttribute("target",whichTarget);
    }
    else{
        theFormObj.removeAttribute("target");
    }
}
```

This function is called from the onBlur event of each text field element in the
Inspector and also from the onChange event of each drop-down list. This way you're
assured that the code will be changed every time the user makes an edit in the Inspector.
The changes are immediate. As soon as the user changes the drop-down list or moves
his cursor from the text field in the Inspector, the edit is made to the document.

If you put this file in the Inspectors folder and restart Dreamweaver, the Inspector
will show itself whenever you select a <form> tag on the page. Figure 4-5 shows
the completed interface for the Form Inspector.

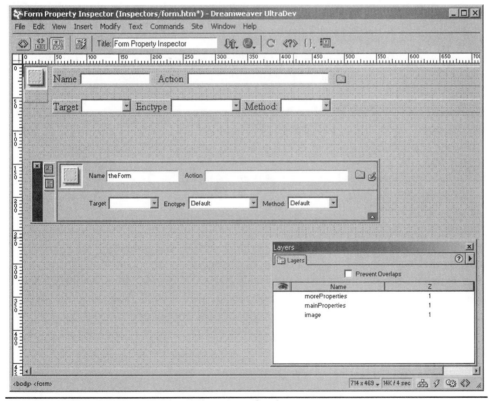

Figure 4-5   *The completed Property Inspector for the <form> tag*

Inspectors can be written for Objects, Server Behaviors, Behaviors, or Data Sources. Although Inspectors are often unnecessary, implementing an Inspector gives your extension a final touch that gives the user an easy way to view and change the properties of an extension.

Floaters

A custom Floater is another form of extension that gives Dreamweaver and UltraDev a unique way to interact with the user. You can use a Floater to incorporate special functionality of your own design into the Dreamweaver environment. A Floater could be described as a modeless command. The restrictions of Inspectors don't apply to Floaters, so you can add as much functionality as you need to the Floater interface. One typical use is to attach a pop-up window to a button in a Property Inspector. This serves to spread out or expand the Inspector, giving the user more room to work with added features in a new window, thereby adding more functionality to the Inspector.

Unlike the other extensions, Floaters don't pop up automatically when dropped into a folder. They have to be invoked by a function call either through a menu item or a button on another extension. You can invoke a Floater by calling `dw.setFloaterVisibility(floatername,true)` or `dw.toggleFloater (floatername)`. The easiest way to do this is by adding a line to the menus.xml file like this:

```
<menuitem name="MyFloater" enabled="true"
command="dw.toggleFloater('MyFloater')"
id="TFM_DWContext_Text_MyFloater" />
```

A menu item like this can be placed anywhere, but a good place for a Floater is in the Window menu on the main menu bar for UltraDev. Floaters can also be put in the contextual menu—if it's something that deserves its own Floater, it's probably something that you will want just a right-click away. The menu item just shown has an ID name, which suggests that it might be under the DWContext_Text menu, the main document contextual menu. We'll discuss the menus.xml file in the next section.

Creating an HTML Mini Editor

Let's build a simple Floater that will display the currently selected tag's HTML in an interface that will allow you to make changes in the HTML and have the changes reflected immediately. It will be like having a mini HTML source viewer that can be used at any and all times.

Begin by creating a new HTML file called QuickHTMLView.htm and save it in the Floaters folder. Place this code in the document as the interface:

```
<html>
<head>
<title>Quick HTML Editor</title>
<script language="JavaScript">
     //^^your code goes here^^
updateCode(){
}
</script>
</head>
<body>
<form name="theForm">
<textarea name="theCode" cols="45" rows="20"
onBlur="updateCode()"></textarea>
</form>
</body>
</html>
```

Now you need to edit the menus.xml file in the DWMenu_Window section. If you open up the menus.xml file in your text editor you can perform a *find* and search for the following text: <menu name="_Window" id="DWMenu_Window">. This will display the main Window menu of Dreamweaver and you'll be able to see all of the menu items that are currently in the menu. Place the following line at the bottom of that particular menu, before the </menu>:

```
<menuitem name="Quick HTML Editor" enabled="true"
command="dw.toggleFloater('QuickHTMLEditor')"
checked="dw.getFloaterVisibility('QuickHTMLEditor')"
id="TFM_Context_Text_QuickHTML" />
```

CAUTION

Always make a backup of a menu file before you edit it. If you make a change that you can't undo, the program may become unusable and you may have to reinstall. Backing up the menu file eliminates this risk. Dreamweaver already has a backup of the menus.xml file called menus.bak in the Menus folder. Also, Public Domain released an extension that will restore your menu system automatically. It's available from the Exchange.

The *checked* attribute shows your Floater on the menu with a check mark next to the name if it is active in the design environment. After editing the menu in this way, you can close UltraDev and restart it. The Quick HTML Editor menu item should appear. If you click it, the Floater should pop up, ready for your text to be input. At this point, the functionality isn't built in yet, but it's now a working Floater that can be used by itself or docked with the other Floaters.

You've already put the function body for the `updateCode()` function in the file, so fill that in first:

```
function updateCode(){
var theDOM = dw.getDocumentDOM();
if(theDOM){
    var offsets = theDOM.getSelection();
    var theCode = document.theForm.theCode.value;
    theNode = theDOM.offsetsToNode(offsets[0],offsets[1]);
    if(theCode=="" && theNode!=null) {
        theCode = theDOM.documentElement.outerHTML;
    }
    var theContent = theNode.outerHTML;
    if(theContent){
        theNode.outerHTML = theCode;
    }else{
        theDOM.documentElement.outerHTML= theCode;
    }
}
}
```

As you can see, there's nothing here that we haven't gone over before. The code checks to see if the DOM exists and, when it doesn't, the function is skipped. This happens if the user doesn't have any documents open. When the DOM exists, you obtain the currently selected code with the `getSelection()` method of the DOM and then get the current value of the text field ("theCode") of the interface. When these two items are not empty, you set the `outerHTML` of the node to whatever is in the text field. When one of these is empty, there is no currently selected element, so the `outerHTML` of the documentElement is displayed instead.

Half the battle is won—the text from the Floater is now being written to the document.

The next step is to get the code from the document and update the Floater. You'll do this with one of the built-in Floater functions, `selectionChanged()`. This is one of those processor-intensive functions that should only be used when necessary, because Dreamweaver is constantly checking the selection and calling this function

on any change. Use it here because you want the code to be updated as it changes.
Here's the function:

```
function selectionChanged(){
var theDOM = dw.getDocumentDOM();
if(theDOM) {
    var offsets = theDOM.getSelection();
    theNode = theDOM.offsetsToNode(offsets[0],offsets[1]);
    var theContent = theNode.outerHTML;
    if(theContent){
        document.theForm.theCode.value = theContent;
    }else{
    document.theForm.theCode.value=theDOM.documentElement.outerHTML
        }
    }
}
```

This function does the opposite of the `updateCode()` function: it takes
whatever is in the currently selected node and displays the `outerHTML` of that
node. If you save this file and restart Dreamweaver, you'll have a mini editor that
will contain whatever happens to be under the cursor as the currently selected node.
If there's no selection, the entire document will show up in the window.

TIP

*A bug in Dreamweaver 3 and UltraDev 1.0 causes the little question mark icon to be unusable for
the `displayHelp` function. If you want to include a help file for your Floater, you have to
display an image button and call the function from that button. This bug was fixed in DW 4.*

Now the Floater will display the currently selected node and allow you to update
the document from the Floater. Like all Floaters, this one can be toggled on and off
and can be docked with another Floater or set of Floaters. Figure 4-6 shows the
completed Floater docked and in use.

Running Commands from a Floater

A Floater can house a mixture of HTML and JavaScript, just like any other
Dreamweaver extension. What makes it unique is the ability to have the Floater
open at all times and docked with other Floaters. This makes it a prime candidate
to act as an interface to your extensions, allowing you to insert objects and run
commands directly from the Floater.

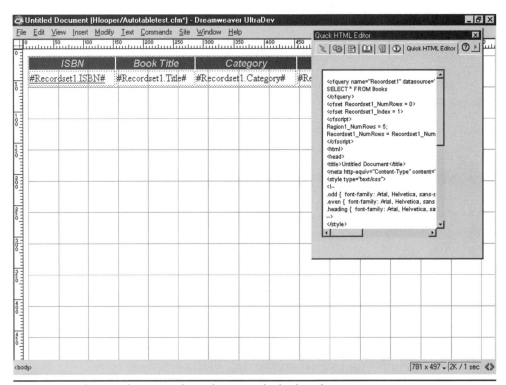

Figure 4-6   *The Quick HTML Editor Floater is docked and in use*

This simple Floater can be adapted to your own environment to run the commands of your choice:

```
<html>
<head>
<title>Test Buttons</title>
<script language="JavaScript">
function isAvailableInCodeView() {
    return true;
}
function isDockable() {
    return false;
}
function isResizable() {
    return false;
}
```

```
function initialTabs() {
    window.resizeTo(150,500);
    return "";
}
</script>
</head>
<body>
<input type="button" name="2Row3Column" value="2 Row 3 Column Table"
onClick="dw.runCommand('Make2Row3ColumnTable')">
<input type="button" name="3Row2Column" value="2 Row 4 Column Table"
onClick="dw.runCommand('Make2Row4ColumnTable')">
<input type="button" name="CSSonPlatform" value="CSS on Platform"
onClick="dw.runCommand('CSS on Platform')">
<input type="button" name="CommentCommands" value="Comment Commands"
onClick="dw.runCommand('Comment Commands')">
</body>
</html>
```

Several new floater API function calls are introduced here. They should be self-explanatory:

▶ **isDockable()**   Is it allowed to dock with other Floaters (true/false)?

▶ **isResizable()**   Is it resizable (true/false)?

▶ **isAvailableInCodeView()**   Is it available in Code view (true/false)?

Also, you'll notice the `initialTabs()` API function. This function is called when the Floater is loaded; this is an ideal time to set the Floater size. The purpose of the `initialTabs()` function is to define where to dock the Floater upon load. You could have specified a return value such as `return "Quick HTML Editor"` to dock it with the previous Floater example. Here, you are simply using the function as a shoehorn to set the Floater size. It's a hack, but some of the best programming techniques are hacks! This technique comes from the Welcome Floater that is included with Dreamweaver.

Obviously, if you can run commands from the Floater, you can do other things as well. You can create a Floater with all of your custom objects on it. UltraDev users can put their custom Server Behavior on a Floater that's accessible from custom icon buttons. Or, you can use a Floater to collect your favorite objects, commands, Server Behaviors, or function calls and make them accessible from your own custom palette of tools. Think of it as a customizable Asset panel.

Creating an Extension Mini Editor

There are some things that are hard to do entirely in the Dreamweaver environment, and extension editing is one of them. If you are working on an extension that has to be tested in the Dreamweaver environment, you must use another program to do it. Then you will have to either restart or reload extensions and continue your debugging. Or you may have to test a snippet of JavaScript. Wouldn't it be convenient to have a hassle-free way to do this? Let's create a Floater that will bring together a few of these operations, as well as introduce a few extension techniques and function calls.

The Extension Mini Editor is actually a very simple Floater that uses the same techniques as the previous two Floaters you created. When the Floater is finished, you'll be able to open any extension file in the Floater, make edits to the file, save it, reload extensions by clicking a button, and reload menus by clicking another button. There will also be a small area that will allow you to type in some JavaScript to be evaluated on-the-fly.

To start with, the main skeleton of the floater is created, along with its user interface:

```
<html>
<head>
<title>Extension Mini Editor</title>
<script language="JavaScript">
//functions here!
</script>
<style type="text/css">
<!--
.text {font-family: Verdana, Arial, Helvetica, sans-serif; font-size: 10px}
-->
</style>

</head>
<body onResize="setTextSize()">
<form name="theForm">
  <table cellspacing="0" cellpadding="0">
    <tr>
      <td nowrap>
        <textarea class="text" name="theCode" style="width:350px;
height:240px"></textarea>
      </td>
      <td nowrap>
        <table cellspacing="0" cellpadding="0">
          <tr>
            <td>
              <input type="image" border="0" name="imageField"
src="../Shared/Basic-UltraDev/Images/duplicate.gif"
```

```
width="22" height="19"
onClick="dw.reloadExtensions();setTextSize(1);">
          </td>
          <td class="text">Reload Extensions</td>
        </tr>
        <tr>
          <td>
            <input type="image" border="0" name="imageField1"
src="../Shared/Basic-UltraDev/Images/duplicate.gif"
width="22" height="19" onClick="dw.reloadMenus()">
          </td>
          <td class="text">Reload Menus</td>
        </tr>
        <tr>
          <td>
            <input type="image" border="0" name="imageField2"
src="../Shared/Basic-UltraDev/images/new.gif"
width="15" height="13" onClick="newExtension()">
          </td>
          <td class="text">New Extension</td>
        </tr>
        <tr>
          <td>
            <input type="image" border="0" name="imageField3"
src="../Shared/Basic-UltraDev/images/browsefolder.gif"
width="15" height="13" onClick="getExtension()">
          </td>
          <td class="text">Load Extension</td>
        </tr>
        <tr>
          <td>
            <input type="image" border="0" name="imageField4"
src="../Shared/Basic-UltraDev/images/save.gif"
width="15" height="13" onClick="saveExtension()">
          </td>
          <td class="text">Save Extension</td>
        </tr>
          <tr>
          <td>
            <input type="image" border="0" name="imageField5"
src="../Shared/Basic-UltraDev/images/trash.gif"
width="15" height="13" onClick="clearWindow()">
          </td>
          <td class="text">Clear Window</td>
        </tr>
      </table>
    </td>
```

```
      </tr>
      <tr>
        <td nowrap>
          <textarea class="text" name="jsEvaluate"
style="width:350px; height:70px"></textarea>
        </td>
        <td>
          <div align="center">
<span class="text">Evaluate some JavaScript</span><br>
            <input type="button" name="Submit" value="Evaluate"
onClick="evaluateTheScript()">
          </div>
        </td>
      </tr>
    </table>
  </form>
  </body>
  </html>
```

This is the complete user interface, which includes two text areas, six image buttons, and one button. Although Macromedia advises against it, the text styles have been set using CSS so that when you reload extensions, the interface won't revert back to Times New Roman. Since the extension includes a Reload Extensions button, this is a necessity. All you need now is some JavaScript to implement the functionality. Start with a global variable:

```
var theFile; //set the global variable for the extension URL
```

This variable will hold the filename and path of the extension file that is currently being edited. Doing this will make the variable available throughout the extension. Next, define a function that will set the size of the text areas within the Floater in the event the user resizes the Floater:

```
function setTextSize(a){
    if(a) window.resizeTo(500,400);
    var winWidth;
    var styleStr;
    if(dreamweaver.getFloaterVisibility("Extension Mini Editor")){
        winWidth = window.innerWidth;
        winHeight = window.innerHeight;
        styleStr = "width:" + (winWidth - 150) + "px";
        findObject('jsEvaluate').style = styleStr;
        styleStr = styleStr + "; height:" + (winHeight - 160) + "px";
        findObject('theCode').style = styleStr;
    }
}
```

If the function is called by using an argument, the window is resized to 500×400. This will happen when the Floater is first loaded. If the function is called with no arguments, the function simply reads the current window height and width and sets the text area sizes accordingly. Notice that only the text area named `theCode` is resized for height. The `jsEvaluate` text area has a static height that was set in the user interface.

Next, some of the common API calls that you've seen before will be incorporated:

```
function isAvailableInCodeView(){
    return true;
}
function isDockable() {
    return false;
}
function initialTabs() {
    setTextSize(1);
    return ""; // don't actually tab with anything else
}
```

These functions don't do anything that we haven't covered in the previous Floater example. However, one obvious change is that the `initialTabs()` function also calls the `setTextSize()` function so that the text areas can be sized proportionally upon load.

Next, here are the functions that will be called from the buttons:

```
function getExtension() {
    theFile = dw.browseForFileURL('select','Choose an
extension',false,true);
    if(DWfile.exists(theFile)){
        var theExtension = DWfile.read(theFile);
        findObject("theCode").value = theExtension;
    }else{
        alert("File doesn't exist");
    }
}
```

This function is set into action when the user clicks Load Extension. The `getExtension()` function gets the filename from the `dw.browseForFileURL()` method and uses a *select* type file dialog box. The other options are *open* and *save*. Also, the next parameter allows you to put a custom message on the file select dialog box. The next option is for bShowPreviewPane, which takes a Boolean value and determines whether the dialog box is going to show an image preview.

Since we're dealing with text files at the moment, you won't need an image preview, so you should use a *false* value. The last parameter is the bSupressSiteRootWarning Boolean attribute. You don't want to be reminded that the file is outside of the site—that's a given—so use a *true* value here.

After thePath variable is returned to the calling function (getExtension()), the DWfile shared C library is called upon to read the file, and the result is placed in the text field named theCode. Notice that you checked to see if the file actually exists prior to reading the file. This is a safety measure to ensure that an error isn't generated.

TIP

DWfile is a shared library that works the same way on Macs and PCs. Through it you can perform file manipulation from within a Dreamweaver extension. Consult the Dreamweaver extensibility documents for a full description of the DWfile API.

The user clicks Save Extension when she has finished editing the extension in the Floater and wants to save the results back to the file. The saveFile() function takes care of this:

```
function saveExtension(){//save the extension
    var theExtension = findObject("theCode").value;
    if(!theFile) {
        alert('Must open an extension')
    }else{
        if(DWfile.write(theFile,theExtension)) {
            alert('Extension saved')
        }else{
            alert('There was an error')
        }
    }
}
```

The contents of the text area named theCode are read into the variable theExtension and then written to the file. Since the variable theFile is a global and holds the name and path of the extension throughout the Floater session, you can use that as the first parameter of the DWfile.write function call, but only if it contains a value. The call to DWfile.write will return a true value if the file-write was successful, so it is best to call it in this manner to check for errors. If the file write fails, an alert box is fired off: "There was an error."

The New Extension button will fire this code, which is similar to the
getExtension() function:

```
function newExtension() {
    theFile = dw.browseForFileURL('save','Create an extension',
        false,true);
    findObject("theCode").value = "";
}
```

The Clear Window button clears the filename from the global variable theFile
and also clears the text field holding the extension:

```
function clearWindow() {
    findObject("theCode").value= "";
    theFile="";
}
```

The Evaluate Script button allows you to write simple JavaScript into the
jsEvaluate text field and have it evaluated. The function that it calls is very simple:

```
function evaluateTheScript() {
    var theScript= findObject("jsEvaluate").value;
    if(theScript) {
        var theEval = eval(theScript);
        alert(theEval)
    }else{
        alert("Enter some JavaScript for evaluation");
    }
}
```

The evaluateTheScript() function uses the JavaScript eval built-in
function to evaluate the contents of the jsEvaluate text field. If the field contains
anything, the eval function will attempt to evaluate it. If not, an alert box will be
called to tell the user to enter some JavaScript. Invalid JavaScript will cause the
function to fail with an error, but the error message will go away after you click
OK and allow you to enter more JavaScript.

There are just two more buttons to account for. These buttons call Dreamweaver
built-in API functions, so they can be called directly from the onClick events of the
image buttons. The Reload Menus button calls the dw.reloadMenus() function,
which will effectively cause Dreamweaver to reload the menu system. This is useful

for extensions that have dynamic menu items or otherwise write to the menus. The Reload Extensions button calls the `dw.reloadExtensions()` function and is similar to holding down the CTRL key and clicking the title bar of the Objects palette. After calling the `dw.reloadExtensions()` function, it calls the `setTextSize()` function using an argument of 1.

CAUTION

Although the `dw.reloadExtensions()` function call is well known in the extensibility community, it is still an as yet undocumented function and doesn't work in all situations.

That completes the Floater example. This was also a very basic Floater, but even with only a few lines of code, it is a fairly powerful extension, allowing you full control over reading, writing, and editing your extension files and having your own mini "immediate" window to evaluate JavaScript. The extension interface is shown in Figure 4-7.

What to Take Away from this Chapter

Inspectors were introduced as a "helper" extension. Property Inspectors don't generally exist as units by themselves, but they enhance the functionality of a program by allowing you quick access to properties of the selected page element. They are also useful for displaying buttons to launch mini editors for the selected tags. Floaters have many uses, and a few of these have been illustrated here, including the ability to edit HTML code from the document, the ability to edit an external file, and its use as a launching pad for other extensions.

Exercises

1. Using the Form Inspector as a guide, build a Car Inspector based on the Car object that was built in Chapter 2.

2. Create a new Floater that launches your three most used objects or commands.

3. Add an Append button to the Extension Mini Editor to append a file to the end of the text currently in the Floater.

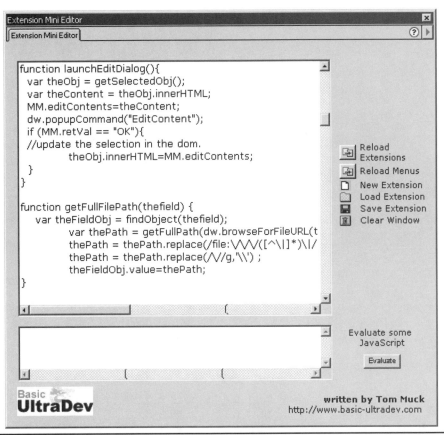

Figure 4-7   *The Extension Mini Editor is a good starting point for your custom Floater extensions*

Introduction to UltraDev Extensions

IN THIS CHAPTER:

How Is UltraDev Different from Dreamweaver?

Extending the Server Behavior Builder (SBB)

Other UltraDev Extensions

What to Take Away from this Chapter

Exercises

S o far in this book, we've focused on Dreamweaver extensions, but at some point you'll probably want to take the leap into UltraDev extensionology. UltraDev is built on Dreamweaver architecture but is much more advanced and allows you to edit ASP, JSP, or ColdFusion pages and add new server models to the program (as a few people have already done with PHP and J2EE 1.2). You can think of UltraDev as the ultimate extension to Dreamweaver.

NOTE

For more coverage of UltraDev extensibility, check out Dreamweaver UltraDev 4: The Complete Reference, also by West and Muck.

How Is UltraDev Different from Dreamweaver?

UltraDev is basically Dreamweaver with extra functionality bolted on. It's kind of like choosing between a car that has none of the added extras versus one that is fully loaded. When you open UltraDev, the only differences you will notice are two extra palettes, Data Bindings and Server Behaviors. These aren't really the only differences, but they are the most obvious. While you can certainly build pages in Dreamweaver that will run ASP, JSP, or ColdFusion, UltraDev allows much greater flexibility because it's able to translate the server-side code into something readable in the design environment. Also, UltraDev allows you the same ease-of-use with server-side code that made Dreamweaver famous for HTML code.

Server Behaviors

Server Behaviors are the snippets of server-side code that can be inserted. Server Behaviors are one of the most advanced extension types, and some of their features include:

▶ They can be inserted in various locations by "weight."

▶ They are recognized and displayed in a palette for future editing.

▶ They can contain numerous code blocks.

▶ They can be written for all four server models included with UltraDev, and any others that may be added later.

These are the steps that UltraDev follows when you select the Server Behavior from the menu and it is applied to a page:

1. The Server Behavior first checks to see if it can be applied (for example, does it need a recordset?). If it can't, it aborts.

   If the page meets the requirements of the Server Behavior, it builds a list of all Server Behaviors of that type, and if necessary, generates unique names for variables and attributes (for example, Repeat1, Repeat2, etc). If not, it aborts.

2. It takes all of the user-defined attributes and inserts them into a mask string. The mask is nothing more than the final code that will be inserted into the page, with masks holding the place of the actual attributes (for example, ##rsname## or @@rsname@@ could hold the place of the actual recordset name that will be used).

3. After the replacements are made in the string, the code is inserted according to *weight*. A description of weights can be found in Table 5-1.

4. After it's inserted, UltraDev will do another search through the document for Server Behaviors to repopulate the list in the Server Behavior palette.

5. The new Server Behavior should appear in the list.

Weight Description	Inserted Where?
0–99 (numbered weights)	Above the HTML tag, relative to any other Server Behavior that has a numbered weight attached to it. A recordset has a weight of 50, so a behavior that executes after a recordset will be between 51 and 99.
aboveHTML+nn	Identical to the above, where *nn* is the weight number. This is new in UltraDev 4. Numbered weights not including this prefix are automatically given the prefix in the SSRecord.
belowHTML+nn	Inserts weighted code below the closing </html> tag, where *nn* is a relative weight between 0 and 99. This was also added in UltraDev 4.
beforeNode	Before the selected node.
afterNode	After the selected node.
replaceNode	Replaces the node with the Server Behavior.

Table 5-1   *The Weights Available to the Server Behavior Programmer*

Weight Description	Inserted Where?
beforeSelection	If there's a selection on the page, inserted before, otherwise, inserted at the insertion point.
afterSelection	If there's a selection on the page, inserted after, otherwise, inserted at the insertion point.
replaceSelection	If there's a selection on the page, replaces the current selection, otherwise, inserted at the insertion point.
afterDocument	Inserted after the closing </html> tag. This weight was used in UltraDev 1 and is converted to belowHTML for backward compatibility.
nodeAttribute+attribname	Sets the attribute for attribname for the node given.
nodeAttribute	Inserts a chunk into the tag after the tag name.

Table 5-1   *The Weights Available to the Server Behavior Programmer* (continued)

Steps for Building a Server Behavior Extension

Unlike Objects, which we covered in Chapter 2, Server Behaviors have several JavaScript functions that must be included in writing the extension. These functions take care of the housekeeping involved in the creation of an instance of a Server Behavior on your page, and they recognize that Server Behavior after it is already applied. Following is the basic framework required to write the extension:

1. You need the final code that you want to use. This should be fully tested code. While you're debugging the Server Behavior, you don't want to worry about whether or not the final code works. After you have a working block of code, you are ready to start building the Server Behavior.

2. Create the actual html file that will act as the user interface for the behavior. This is pretty straightforward and consistent for all extensions. User interfaces have been covered in the preceding chapters.

3. Add your include files to the document. Server Behaviors use a standard set of JavaScript files from the Shared directory.

4. Set some other global variables that are needed for the behavior, including the code weight.

5. Include the `initializeUI()` function. This will set up the user interface if it requires any information such as recordsets.

6. Add a search string at the top of the file. This will be a simple, unique string that is found in your code. It acts as a scout for the behavior. When you apply any edits to your document, UltraDev will look for the search string in your document; if it doesn't find it, it won't even bother to check for an instance of the behavior.

7. Write the pattern and mask variables for your code. The pattern code is a regular expression pattern used to find the code in the document, and the mask variable is your actual code to be inserted, with masks in place of your user-defined attributes.

8. Write function skeletons for the five Server Behavior functions and any other functions that you may need:

   ▶ **canApplyServerBehavior()**   Checks to make sure that the page has the necessary ingredients for the Server Behavior. If you're editing an existing instance of a Server Behavior, the function takes an SSRecord object as an argument.

   ▶ **findServerBehaviors()**   Returns an array of SSRecord object instances on the page.

   ▶ **applyServerBehavior()**   Inserts the behavior onto the page. If you're editing an existing instance of a Server Behavior, the function takes an SSRecord as an argument.

   ▶ **inspectServerBehavior()**   Takes an SSRecord as an argument and updates the behavior's user interface to reflect the parameters of the behavior.

   ▶ **deleteServerBehavior()**   Takes an SSRecord as an argument and deletes the SB from the page.

9. Implement each of the required functions in turn, and any supporting functions. If you're writing the functions by hand, you should test them along the way, making sure each part does what it's supposed to do up until that point.

10. Implement the analyzeServerBehavior function, if needed. This function performs a couple of tasks, making sure the node is in fact an instance of your behavior and setting certain properties in the SSRecord (including the incomplete property, selectedNode property, title property, and participants property).

11. Implement, if needed, `copyServerBehavior` and `pasteServerBehavior`. These are only necessary if you want your user to be able to copy and paste the behaviors into the same document or another document.

As you can see, it's quite a bit more complex than putting an object into your document. If this task seems a little daunting at first glance, there is some good news. In UltraDev 4, a new feature called the Server Behavior Builder (SBB) was introduced. The SBB performs most of these steps automatically for you—except for step 1, of course, and a couple of the optional steps. We will concentrate on using the SBB and create a simple Server Behavior for ASP/VBScript.

Your Final Code: The First Step

You'll begin at the end with the code that you want to be inserted in the page by the Server Behavior. You'll build a Server Behavior that allows a user to download the output of a Repeated Region as a text file. We've chosen this particular Server Behavior for the following reasons:

▶ It has more than one code block. Building Server Behaviors with the SBB makes it easy to implement multiple code blocks.

▶ The code blocks demonstrate three different weights.

▶ There is only one parameter, a plain text field that you'll modify later to validate the user input.

▶ It can be easily adapted to another server model, such as ColdFusion or JSP.

The code for the behavior is as follows. To keep it simple, we'll call the code blocks block1, block2, and block3, although in actual practice you should name your blocks with meaningful names. The SBB will give the blocks default names of *ServerBehaviorName_blockN* when creating the new blocks. The first block will be inserted at the top of the file, right below the language declaration.

```
<%Response.Buffer="true"%>
```

The second block will be inserted *before* the user selection:

```
<%
Response.Clear()
Response.AddHeader "Content-Disposition","inline; filename=@@Filename@@"
Response.ContentType = "application/unknown"
'Basic-ultradev DownloadRepeatRegion Server Behavior
%>
```

And finally, a closing code block will be inserted *after* the user selection:

```
<%
Response.Flush()
Response.End()
%>
```

Accessing the Server Behavior Builder (SBB)

Start by opening a site in UltraDev that is ASP/VBScript. Open the SBB by clicking Plus (+) in the Server Behavior palette. At the bottom of the palette are three choices—New Server Behavior, Edit Server Behavior, and Get More Server Behaviors. Click New Server Behavior (see Figure 5-1), which will bring you to the dialog box shown in Figure 5-2.

This is where you give the Server Behavior a name, set the language that you want to use, and choose whether you want to copy an existing Server Behavior. Call this Server Behavior DownloadRepeatRegion and make it ASP/VBScript. Leave the Option check box unchecked, since this is a new Server Behavior.

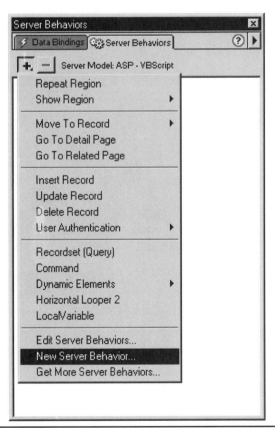

Figure 5-1   *The SBB is invoked by clicking New Server Behavior or Edit Server Behaviors*

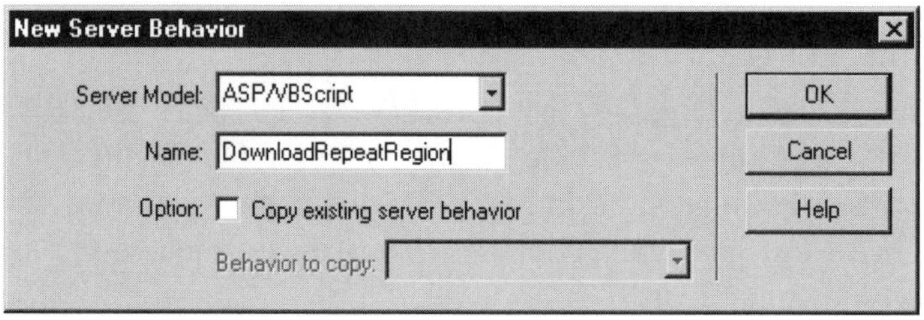

Figure 5-2   *The first dialog box of the SBB*

Click OK to see the following dialog box:

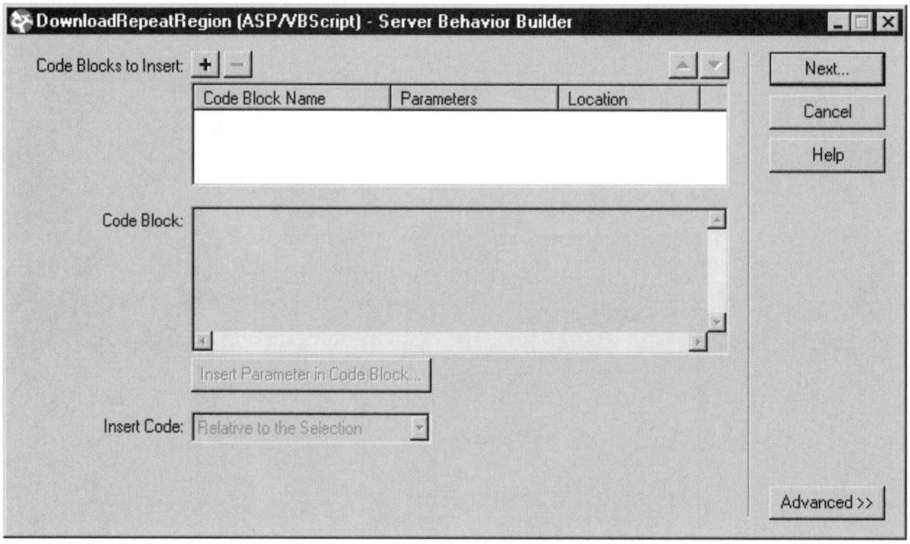

This is the main window of the SBB. The first thing you should do is to click the Advanced button to open up the window to the advanced functionality. If you don't perform this step, possible errors can occur, which we'll explain shortly. This will bring up the next dialog box, now expanded:

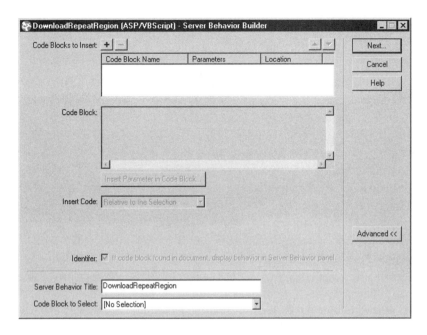

By doing this you are now allowed to choose an identifying code block, which is a necessity in an extension like this. Whenever your extension contains a block of code that could be misconstrued by another participating Server Behavior, you want to make sure that the code block is not checked as an identifier. In this case, block1 and block3 could easily be participants of other Server Behaviors.

Creating the Code Blocks

To create the code blocks, you have to click Plus (+) in the dialog box for each code block in turn. All code blocks must be inserted before clicking the Next button in the dialog box. Since you are using the default name of block1, it will show up in the window as DownloadRepeatRegion_block1.

The first block is the `<%Response.Buffer="true"%>` line. There are no parameters for this block. This is an ASP statement that has to be placed immediately after the language declaration before any headers are sent to the browser and before any other ASP code is executed. This can be done by assigning the code a numbered weight that will place it before any other code blocks. Code weights are taken care of automatically by the SBB. In the Insert Code drop-down box you should choose Above the <html> tag. Then, in the Relative Position drop-down box, you should choose The Beginning of the File. This ensures that the code block is placed right after the language declaration. You'll notice that the actual code weight is listed next to this drop-down box and is grayed out. If you had chosen Custom Position, you could have designated in your own numbered code weight. In this case, the numbered weight is 1.

For this code block, make sure that you uncheck the Identifier check box. If the Identifier box were checked, this Server Behavior would erroneously show up whenever the <%Response.Buffer="true"%> line was on a page. Checking this box is a frequent mistake made by people creating Server Behaviors for the first time.

Next, block2 is added in the same manner. Click Plus (+) in the dialog box and create block2. Block2 is your main identifying code block, so check the Identifier check box in this case. Add a comment at the end of the block to make sure that another Server Behavior won't misinterpret the code block as one of its participants. The code block once again looks like this:

```
<%
Response.Clear()
Response.AddHeader "Content-Disposition","inline;
filename=@@Filename@@"
Response.ContentType = "application/unknown"
'Basic-ultradev DownloadRepeatRegion Server Behavior
%>
```

The double @ signs surround your parameter. You can type these in manually, or you can let the SBB do it for you by selecting the text that you want to replace with a parameter and then clicking the Insert Parameter in Code Block button. This will insert your parameter and automatically put @@ around the name.

Parameter names are later used in the extension interface, so you should name your parameters carefully to avoid having to adjust your interface by hand. You can't always do this, but you should take advantage of every timesaving procedure you can find. The example is named Filename with a capital *F* so that it shows up nicely in the interface.

This code block will be inserted relative to the user's selection on the page. As shown in Table 5-1, there are several weights that can be used that deal with selections. Choose Relative to the Selection in the Insert Code drop-down box and then choose Before the Selection in the Relative Position drop-down box. Once again, the SBB will take care of all of the details of inserting the code relative to the selection, and no JavaScript coding is necessary.

NOTE

The SBB automates the process of building Server Behaviors, but it doesn't really change the way that the extension is written. It simply generates the HTML, JavaScript, and XML files necessary for the Server Behavior by using a template. UltraDev 4 has a new XML extensibility architecture, but it's not tied directly to the SBB. You can write the XML files by hand also.

Another thing that you'll notice about this code block is that the Server Behavior Title text field at the bottom of the dialog box now contains a parameter as part of the title. This is the title that you see when the Server Behavior is added to the page and shown in the Server Behavior palette. In this case, leave it as it stands, but in the case of a Server Behavior with numerous parameters, you can edit the title so that it's not too long to be displayed in the Server Behavior palette by removing extraneous parameters from the title and leaving in only the parameters that make sense to have in the title.

Code block3 is the last code block that you'll be using for this Server Behavior. Like the other code blocks, this is a fairly simple block that could be easily found in another Server Behavior, so make sure that the Identifier check box is unchecked. Again, this code block will be inserted relative to the user's selection on the page. Choose Relative to the Selection in the Insert Code drop-down box and then choose After the Selection in the Relative Position drop-down box. Once again, the SBB will take care of all of the details of inserting the code relative to the selection.

One last step and the code blocks will be finished: choose which block will be selected when the Server Behavior is selected in the Server Behavior palette. To do this, choose DownloadRepeatRegion_block2 from the Code Block to Select drop-down box on the bottom of the dialog box. Now, whenever the behavior is chosen in the Server Behaviors palette, the block of ASP code on the page will be selected in Code view or in Design view.

Generating the Interface

With the code blocks out of the way, you can now click the Next button to take you to the next step, which generates the HTML interface. The interface that is generated is stored in the ServerBehaviors folder under the server model that you are working with. For this example, it will be stored in the ASP folder.

This HTML file can be manipulated manually after the Server Behavior is built. It follows all of the same guidelines as the other extension types that we've dealt with. One thing you need to be aware of, however, is that if you later choose to edit the Server Behavior with the SBB, the HTML interface will be overwritten and your changes will be lost. It's always a good idea to keep backups of everything as you are working on the Server Behavior.

After clicking Next, you are taken to the following dialog box:

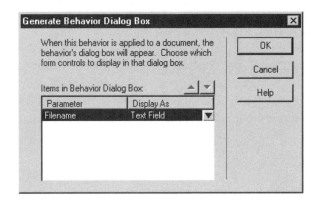

The parameter that you are inserting can use a plain text field for the user input. The standard controls are as follows:

▶ **Text Field**   Plain text field.

▶ **Dynamic Text Field**   Plain text field with a dynamic button next to it, which allows the use of dynamic text items, such as Session variables.

▶ **Recordset Menu**   Shows a drop-down list of available recordsets on the page.

▶ **Recordset Field Menu**   Shows a drop-down list of recordset field names.

▶ **URL Text Field**   Allows you to choose a relative or absolute file URL.

▶ **Tag Menu**   Special item that is needed when your code block depends on a specific tag.

When you are done with this step, click OK and the Server Behavior is finished—or as finished as it can be using the SBB. As mentioned previously, the SBB only creates the behavior based on a standard template, and there is some functionality still missing. The next section will deal with that, but first, it's time to try out the behavior.

The Server Behavior that you just built will allow the user browsing the page to download the output of a Repeat Region as a file. This has many uses, such as dumping the contents of a search, the results of a test, or raw data from a database. You can save the file as a plain text file or as a .csv file. The page has to be set up properly first.

For this simple example, use the Scaal Coffee example that ships with UltraDev and declare a recordset using this SQL statement:

```
SELECT fOwner, fPhone
FROM Franchises
```

For the sake of brevity, we'll assume that you know how to create recordsets and Repeat Regions in UltraDev. Given that, put the fOwner and fPhone columns on the page (not inside a table, as you may have done before). Put a comma between the two columns. One last thing to do is to go into code view and add a line feed/carriage return after the second column. This can be done with the following VBScript statement:

```
<%=vbCrLf%>
```

This is a standard VBScript variable that includes a carriage return and a line feed character (chr(13) and chr(10)). The whole thing should look like this (all on one line in UltraDev):

```
<%=(Recordset1.Fields.Item("fOwner").Value)%>,
<%=(Recordset1.Fields.Item("fPhone").Value)%><%=vbCrLf%>
```

Next, you can highlight the entire region in Design view or Code view and apply a Repeat Region to it showing all records. Next, simply apply the new behavior to the entire region, give the file a name like test.txt, and browse the page. The page should pop up a dialog box to download the test.txt file. After downloading the file, you can open it up. You should see something like this in the file:

Adam Eve,949 568 7852

Austin Anderson,213 765 6545

Doris Molly Graham,520 233 0512

Bill Szeto,528 613 0391

and so on.

This was just a simple example; you should be able to figure out many possible uses for this Server Behavior.

Adding JavaScript to the Auto-Generated File

You may immediately notice that there is no validation performed on the user-input when you build a Server Behavior with the SBB. At the very least, you should include some JavaScript code to verify that something was entered. If you remember the previously mentioned Server Behavior steps, step 8 sounds like the perfect place to intercept and validate the user input before applying the SB to the page. The `applyServerBehavior():` function does the work of inserting the behavior onto the page.

This is the function you'll have to find in the HTML file so that you can intercept the code before it is inserted and verify that the user has input something. Open up the DownloadRepeatRegion.htm file located in the Configuration | ServerBehaviors | ASP folder. The `applyServerBehavior()` function looks like this for this behavior:

```
function applyServerBehavior(sbObj) {
    var paramObj = new Object();
    var errStr = "";
    if (!errStr)
        errStr = _Filename.applyServerBehavior(sbObj, paramObj);
    if (!errStr) {
        fixUpSelection(dw.getDocumentDOM(), true, true;
        applySB(paramObj, sbObj)
    }
    return errStr;
}
```

You can see that there is a variable named *errStr* that controls whether anything happens in the behavior. If there is something in *errStr*, the SB isn't applied and *errStr* is returned from the function. However, it's not clear from this what happens to *errStr*.

The variable *errStr* actually shows up as an alert box if it contains a string value, so the best way to prevent the `applyServerBehavior()` function from firing is to set *errStr* to an error message to be displayed to the user. You can do that by adding a line right after the *errStr* definition:

```
if(findObject("Filename").value =="") errStr = "You must enter a value";
```

That will do the trick. If you save the file now with this change and restart UltraDev, you can try it out. The behavior won't allow you to apply it if you don't enter something in the Filename box.

XML Files

UltraDev 4 has a new architecture for Server Behaviors and translators that
uses XML files. These aren't true XML files but rather are a special format that
Dreamweaver and UltraDev can understand. You should use a regular text editor on
these files because a dedicated XML editor might fail on some of the syntax. The
XML files contain the code that is to be inserted by the Server Behavior and also the
patterns used to match the Server Behavior on the page. We'll describe some of the
key points, but for a full explanation of the XML architecture, you should read the
extensibility documents that come with UltraDev and are available from
Macromedia in a bound volume.

The files are located in the Configuration | ExtensionData folder. Typically there
is a main Group file and then a Participant file for each of the code blocks that were
created. The Group file contains general information about the Participant files. This
is always named with the same name as your Server Behavior. In this case, it's named
DownloadRepeatRegion.xml. The file looks like this:

```
<group name="DownloadRepeatRegion"
serverBehavior="DownloadRepeatRegion.htm">
<title>DownloadRepeatRegion (@@Filename@@)</title>
<groupparticipants selectParticipant="DownloadRepeatRegion_block2">
    <groupparticipant name="DownloadRepeatRegion_block1"
     partType="member" />
    <groupparticipant name="DownloadRepeatRegion_block2"
     partType="identifier" />
    <groupparticipant name="DownloadRepeatRegion_block3"
     partType="member" />
</groupparticipants>
</group>
```

As you can see, the XML tags are pretty easy to understand. The *name* attribute
shows the name of the Server Behavior, and the *serverBehavior* attribute shows
the actual Server Behavior file. The `<groupParticipants>` tag contains the
selectParticipant attribute, which is the name of the participant that causes the code
to become selected in the design environment when the user selects the Server
Behavior in the Server Behavior palette. The `<groupParticipant>` tags
are child tags of the `<groupParticipants>` tag and list the names of the various
participants of the extension. The names are equal to the XML participant files minus
the .xml file extension.

The file can also be changed manually, and any changes you make in the file will show up the next time you open it up in the SBB. Once again, though, if you make any manual changes in any of the files generated by the SBB, including the XML files, the changes will be lost once you edit the behavior with the SBB.

The participant files are where you will probably be making most of your changes, if you have to change anything. There are many reasons for making changes, but the foremost reason is to change the pattern. We've mentioned regular expressions in the preceding chapters, but when you are dealing with Server Behaviors, it becomes imperative that you fully understand and are fluent in the creation of regular expressions.

The patterns generated by the SBB are good and work well for the stock behaviors. As soon as an element of hand-coding is entered, however, the pattern generated by the SBB will fail because it's always looking for an exact match. Programming is not an exact science, and code can be modified by you or other users in ways that you might not have considered when you originally built the behavior.

Let's take the second block as an example. This is the participant XML file in its entirety:

```
<participant name="DownloadRepeatRegion_block2">
<implementation serverModel="ASP/VBScript">
<insertText location="beforeSelection"><![CDATA[<%
Response.Clear()
Response.AddHeader "Content-Disposition","inline;
filename=@@Filename@@"
Response.ContentType = "application/unknown"
'Basic-ultradev DownloadRepeatRegion Server Behavior
%>
]]></insertText>
<searchPatterns whereToSearch="directive">
 <searchPattern paramNames="Filename" limitSearch="all">
 <![CDATA[/<%\s*Response\.Clear\(\)\s*Response\.AddHeader\s*"Content-
 Disposition","inline;\s*filename=(.*)"\s*Response\.ContentType\s*=
 \s*"application\/unknown"\s*'Basic-ultradev\s*DownloadRepeatRegion
 \s*Server\s*Behavior\s*%>/i]]>
 </searchPattern>
</searchPatterns>
<quickSearch>"Content-Disposition","inline;</quickSearch>
</implementation>
</participant>
```

The main tag is the <participant> tag, which gives the name of the participant. Beneath that, is the <implementation> tag, which lists the name of the server model for which the participant is used. If you have implemented a Server Behavior with more than one server model, you might have multiple <implementation> tags in one XML participant file.

The <quickSearch> tag acts like a quick glance through the document to find an instance of your behavior. In a manually created Server Behavior with just HTML and JavaScript, you can use a search string comment tag at the top of the HTML Server Behavior file to act as your quick search. If UltraDev doesn't find the <quickSearch> string in the document, it knows that a more thorough search for the Server Behavior is not required.

Next, the <insertText> tag contains the code that is being inserted and tells UltraDev where to put the code. The code contained within this tag is the actual code that will be inserted into the document, exactly as you entered it in the SBB, with the user-defined attributes masked out. In the hand-coded HTML and JavaScript Server Behaviors of UltraDev 1, these were the MASK variables. With the knowledge of how the MASK variables of UltraDev 1 work, you can create these masks used in the <insertText> tags manually as well.

The <searchPattern> tags contain information about the regular expression pattern that is used to find the code in the user's document. These patterns were the PATT variables in the hand-coded UltraDev 1 Server Behaviors. With the knowledge of how these pattern variables are built, you can build your own from scratch or modify the patterns created by the SBB to make them more efficient. The <searchPattern> tag also contains a list of the parameters that were defined in the SBB. The <searchPattern> tag is contained within a <searchPatterns> tag, allowing the use of several pattern blocks to be used by defining separate <searchPattern> tags for each one.

Your first little bit of hand-coding is with the <quickSearch> tag. In the stock Server Behavior straight from the SBB, the <quickSearch> tag looks like this:

```
<quickSearch>"Content-Disposition","inline;</quickSearch>
```

That might seem like a perfectly reasonable quick-search. The <quickSearch> tag only checks to see if there is any reason for UltraDev to look for a Server Behavior on that particular page. You can narrow it down a little more, however, by putting something in the <quickSearch> tag that will *only* be in this behavior—part of the comment:

```
<quickSearch>DownloadRepeatRegion</quickSearch>
```

That's the first change, but you're not done yet. The regular expression pattern is your primary concern. A pattern generated by the builder will only find an exact match, but you want to make it a little more fuzzy so that any hand-coding won't interfere with the recognition of the Server Behavior. More importantly, you want to make sure that any hand-coding won't get lost if you make an edit in the Server Behavior.

First, take the pattern and break it down into two different `<searchPattern>` tags. One thing that you have to understand about matching a node is that UltraDev will grab the entire node for you. The `<searchPattern>` tag only has to match a small part of that node for a match to be found. For example, if your node looks like this:

```
<%Response.Write("hello there")
'Tom's node «-- %>
```

your `<searchPattern>` tag would find a match if it looked like this:

```
<searchPattern limitSearch="all"><![CDATA[/'Tom/i]]></searchPattern>
```

In other words, it keys on the match within the node and doesn't have to match the entire node. This is the key to hand-coding your `<searchPattern>` tags.

With that in mind, you should break the `<searchPattern>` tag into two smaller units:

```
<searchPattern limitSearch="all">
<![CDATA[/DownloadRepeatRegion\s*Server\s*Behavior\s*%>/i]]>
</searchPattern>
<searchPattern paramNames="Filename" limitSearch="all">
<![CDATA[/"Content-Disposition","inline;\s*filename=([^"]*)"/i]]>
</searchPattern>
```

The first pattern matches the comment you inserted. This is to ensure that only your Server Behavior will be found. The second `<searchPattern>` is included because it has an attribute that has to be matched: the Filename. If you run the Server Behavior at this point, half the battle will be won. The patterns will be much more flexible now, and the Server Behavior will still show up in the palette even if some hand-coding is introduced to the code block.

One final bit of hand-coding is necessary to allow the update of the Server Behavior while keeping any other hand-coding intact. This involves the use of the `<updatePattern>` tag. This special tag is not generated by the SBB for any reason but should always be hand-coded into your Server Behavior so that the behavior will be more flexible and allow hand-coding.

The <updatePattern> tag is enclosed within a set of <updatePatterns> opening and closing tags. The tag is included so that a portion of the node can be updated without affecting the rest of the node. This is accomplished, once again, with a regular expression—in fact, the same regular expression that was used in the second <searchPattern> tag. The entire tag set looks like this:

```
<updatePatterns>
<updatePattern paramName="Filename">
<![CDATA[/("Content-Disposition","inline;\s*filename=)[^"]*(")/i]]>
</updatePattern>
</updatePatterns>
```

When you use the Server Behavior now, you can include hand-coding within code block2, and it will be maintained even if you edit the Server Behavior.

Extending the Server Behavior Builder (SBB)

In keeping with the tradition of extensibility, Macromedia also made the SBB in UltraDev extensible. You can extend the SBB by changing the ServerBehaviorTemplate.asp file located in Configuration | Shared | Controls. This template, upon examination, is actually JavaScript. If you've looked at a few Server Behaviors generated by the SBB, you'll see exactly where they came from—the ServerBehaviorTemplate.asp. While it's beyond the scope of this book to delve too deeply into customizing this template, we'll show you a simple change you can make to include your own logo into the files generated by the SBB.

CAUTION

If you want to modify the ServerBehaviorTemplate.asp file, it is strongly suggested you make a backup copy of the original file and keep it in a safe place. If the original file is damaged, the SBB won't work anymore.

If you open up that file (ServerBehaviorTemplate.asp) and look inside the <body> tags of the document, it looks like this:

```
<BODY onLoad="initializeUI()">
<% if (numParameters > 0) { %>
<FORM NAME="theForm">
  <TABLE BORDER=0>
<% for (i = 0; i < numParameters; i++) { %>
```

```
    <TR>
     <TD ALIGN="right" VALIGN="baseline" NOWRAP>
      <%= paramLabels[i] %>:
     </TD>
     <TD VALIGN="baseline" NOWRAP>
      <%= paramControlSources[i].replace(/\n/g, "\n          ") %>
     </TD>
    </TR>
<% } %>
</TABLE>
</FORM>
<% } %>
</BODY>
```

The code is easy to understand and easily modified. First, the <body> tag is written to the Server Behavior file with an event: initializeIU(). Next, if there are parameters, a form is written to the server behavior. If not, the closing </body> tag is written.

Just by looking at the looping code in the code listing, you should be able to tell that the parameters are each inserted into a separate table row. You can easily sneak your own logo into a row of its own after the parameters loop has ended. Right after the closing <% } %> tag, you can insert your logo with a link to your home page in one row and a brief description in another row:

```
<tr bgcolor="#d3d3d3">
  <td align="left" valign="baseline" colspan="2">
    Insert a <%= serverBehaviorTitle %> SB on the page.
  </td>
</tr>
<tr bgcolor="#d3d3d3">
  <td align = "left">
  <input type="image"
   src="../../Shared/basic-ultradev/images/smBD.gif"
onClick='dreamweaver.browseDocument("http://www.basic-ultradev.com")'>
  </td>
  <td align="right" valign="baseline" nowrap><br>
   <b>written by Tom Muck</b><br>
   http://www.basic-ultradev.com
  </td>
</tr>
```

Most of this is self-explanatory, but the one thing that you may not have noticed is this:

```
<%= serverBehaviorTitle %>
```

As you can see, the ServerBehaviorTemplate.asp file uses ASP JavaScript!

Another way you can extend the SBB is by building your own controls. The main controls for the SBB are located in Configuration | Shared | Controls | String Menu. These are the HTML files that the SBB uses to populate the drop-down list of available controls. You can easily add a new one by copying an existing control file and making changes in it.

The interface of the control is in the HTML file, but the functionality is in the JavaScript file located in Configuration | Shared | Controls | Scripts. If you add your own control to the SBB, you have to make sure you include the .js file of the new control in your Server Behavior package if you distribute it.

The standard controls are these:

► **Text Field**   Allows any text input.

► **Dynamic Text Field**   Allows text or a dynamic text item.

► **Recordset Menu**   Drop-down list of recordsets.

► **Recordset Field Menu**   Drop-down list of recordset fields.

► **URL Text Field**   A text field with a browse button to allow insertion of a link to a file or page.

► **Tag Menu**   Drop-down list of a particular tag on the page.

As you can see, there are not too many choices, but the SBB, like UltraDev itself, is extensible. Figure 5-3 shows a SBB that has been extended with a few extra controls. We'll guide you through building a very simple control based on the standard text field: a color picker. Building the extension will add the Dreamweaver Color Picker control to the standard drop-down list of available SBB controls.

Since this file will be modified from the existing text field, we'll just highlight the changes. First, make a copy of the text field.htm file located in Configuration | Shared | Controls | String Menu. These files contain a reference to the JavaScript file that contains the functionality, as well as the all code that will be used in the final Server Behavior. Like the ServerBehaviorTemplate.asp file that was just shown, this

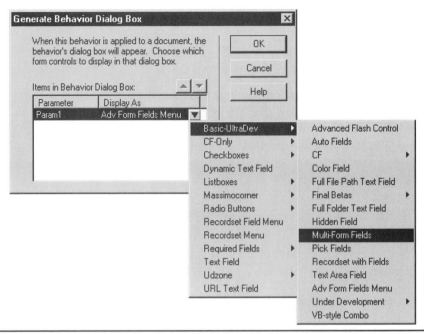

Figure 5-3   *The standard SBB has six controls; this one has a few more*

file has variables in it that will be filled in by the SBB. You could say that these controls extend the ServerBehaviorTemplate.asp file, not UltraDev itself.

The control file consists of two functions: `controlFiles()` and `controlSource()`. The `controlFiles()` function is an array of paths to shared JavaScript files that the control needs in order to work. In this case, there is only one file reference, but you can include as many as your control requires. The `controlSource()` function builds the HTML that is needed for the Server Behavior interface much like the `objectTag()` function does in the Object extensions. The control name is substituted for all instances of the variable *name* in the function. The return value is the completed HTML control.

TIP

The Server Behavior Control extensions, like Server Behaviors, can also be placed into their own folders under the String Menu folder for better organization.

Three changes need to be made to the text field.htm file:

```
<TITLE>Text Field</TITLE>
```

needs to be changed to

```
<title>Color Field</title>
```

Next, this line:

```
"Shared/Controls/Scripts/TextField.js");
```

needs to be changed to

```
"Shared/Controls/Scripts/ColorField.js");
```

Finally, the `controlSource()` function needs to replaced with the following:

```
function controlSource(name) {
  return '' +
    '<input type="mmcolorbutton" name="' + name + 'color"
    onChange="findObject(' + "'" + name + "'" +
    ').value=this.value"><input type="text" name="' +
    name + '" size="26" onBlur="findObject(' + "'" +
    name + "color'" + ").value=this.value>"';
}
```

The `controlSource()` function is the actual string that will be inserted in your Server Behavior when you build it with the SBB and choose the ColorField as your input source. As you can see, just as in the ServerBehaviorTemplate.asp file, there are variables in this function that are going to be replaced by the SBB. In this case, the string is returned to the SBB after the *name* variable has been replaced in this function four times and the string has been concatenated.

Now, you'll need to make a copy of the TextField.js file located in Configuration | Shared | Controls | Scripts. Name this one ColorField.js. The first thing you'll need to do to this copy of the original file is a global find/replace on all instances of the word TextField, replacing it with ColorField. Next, add the functionality to read the mmcolorcontrol and return the value to the Server Behavior using this control. This is done in three separate functions:

In the `ColorField_initializeUI()` function, add this line right after the similar line for the text field:

```
this.colorControl = findObject(this.paramName+'color');
```

In the `ColorField_inspectServerBehavior()` function, add this line right after the similar line for the text field:

```
this.colorControl.value = theValue;
```

Finally, in the `ColorField_setValue()` function, add this line right after the similar line for the text field:

```
this.colorControl.value = theValue;
```

That's all there is to it for the new ColorField Server Behavior control. The Server Behavior that you build with this control will read the value from the text field—the color picker is simply there to set the value of the text field. The text field also has the ability to set the value of the color picker. That is, if you change the value of the color in the text field itself, the color in the color picker will change. You can now use this control in any server behavior that you build that may need to have a color attribute assigned somewhere in the behavior, such as in an alternate colored row extension.

Other UltraDev Extensions

This chapter is intended to be a general overview of UltraDev extensions, with a focus on Server Behaviors. Some of the other UltraDev extension types that are available to you are as follows:

Data Sources

These extensions, available from the Data Bindings palette in UltraDev, are some of the more complex examples of extensions available. They are generally tied in with commands and Server Behaviors. A good example of a Data Source extension is the UltraDev Shopping Cart, which shows up in the Server Behavior palette when applied but also shows up as a Data Source in the Data Bindings palette. Data Sources generally available as items that can be inserted on the page display a server-side variable or the result of executing server-side code to the final page. Recordsets, variables, cookies, COM objects, CF tags, and shopping carts are all examples of Data Sources.

The Data Source extensions are located in the DataSources folder and can be written from scratch using HTML and JavaScript or modified from existing Data Sources.

Connections

The connection extension is what you find if you click Modify | Connections to bring up a new connection dialog box. Currently, in ASP you have an ODBC data source and a Custom Connection String, but you can easily create your own connection extension that might have a different type of connection method, or perhaps a more automatic method of creating an ADO connection string. The JSP connection files are more easily adapted to create connection files for different JDBC drivers.

To create your own JSP connection extension for a driver that isn't listed, which is a simple HTML file in this case, open the Configuration | Connections | JSP folder and then open the Mac or Win folder, depending on which machine you're using. In that folder are the interface files (dialog boxes) for the various connections that are implemented in UltraDev. To create the dialog box for a driver that isn't listed, you'll have to create your own interface for the driver. The following are the general steps you must follow to create the driver interface:

1. Copy one of the other driver files, such as the db2app_jdbc_conn.htm file, and open it in Notepad or your text editor of choice.

2. Change the `<title>` tag to reflect your new driver name. In this example, the JDataConnect driver, from NetDirect is used. `<title>JDataConnect JDBC Driver</title>`

3. Find the global variables section and replace the individual variables with your own driver information:

```
//Global Variables
var DEFAULT_DRIVER = "JData2_0.sql.$Driver";
var
DEFAULT_TEMPLATE="jdbc:JDataConnect://[hostname:port]/[odbc]";
var MSG_DriverNotFound = "JDataConnect Driver not found!";
var FILENAME = "JDataConnect_jdbc_conn.htm";
```

4. Save the file with the filename used in the FILENAME variable in the proper folder (Win or Mac).

5. Restart UltraDev and create a new connection by clicking Modify | Connections and clicking New. Your new driver should appear.

The DEFAULT_DRIVER variable is the driver name that will appear in the Driver text field when you create the new connection. The DEFAULT_TEMPLATE variable is the URL of the driver that acts as a template, with brackets surrounding information that the user can supply. The MSG_DriverNotFound variable is the error message that will be displayed if an error occurs. The FILENAME variable is the present connection file's name.

Server Formats

Server Format extensions are the data formatting code that you can apply to a data source that will apply formats such as money, date, time, or capitalization to your server-side code. Server Formats can also be written from scratch using HTML and JavaScript or modified from existing Server Format files. In addition, you need to modify the Formats.xml file located in the ServerFormats folder to add your format to the menu along with a regular expression used to find the code for your format on the page.

These extensions are built a little differently than some of the other extensions, since you must insert a RegExp pattern right in the menu file. Like the regular expressions that are in the Server Behaviors, this expression is used by UltraDev to match the format in the code on your page. It is best to edit this menu file manually and insert your code.

There are three folders within the Server Formats folder that correspond with the three server models that work with UltraDev—ASP, JSP, and ColdFusion. Each of these folders has a corresponding Formats.xml menu file as well, which is the menu where your changes will go.

The extensions are fairly consistent. You can easily take an existing Server Format and change it to reflect the new format that you want to implement. You'll find that most of the Server Formats contain three basic functions: formatDynamicDataRef, applyFormat, and deleteFormat. In addition, some of the Server Formats will write a function to the head of the user's document. In those cases, a fourth function will build a string that contains the text of the function.

Server Models

Currently, UltraDev offers support for ASP 2.0, JSP 1.0, and ColdFusion 4.0, but you can add a new ServerModel extension so that UltraDev could support another server type such as PHP 3, PHP 4, CF 5, ASP 3, JSP 1.1, or any other server-side technology. As of this writing, there is a popular PHP 4.0 Server Model available for UltraDev 4, as well as a JSP 1.1 Server Model. Server Model extensions are not to be taken lightly, as you will have to implement the entire code structure of UltraDev for the server that you want to support.

What to Take Away from this Chapter

Extensions are additions to Dreamweaver's functionality. UltraDev was introduced as the ultimate extension to Dreamweaver. You learned the steps for building Server Behaviors by building one using a new feature of UltraDev 4—the Server Behavior Builder. You learned that the SBB used a template behind the scenes and that it could be modified. The SBB can be extended with new controls, and the basics of building controls were outlined. Finally, several other UltraDev extension types were described briefly as an introduction to the world of UltraDev extensibility.

Exercises

1. Change the validation for the Filename text field in our sample Server Behavior (DownloadRepeatRegion) so that it only accepts valid filenames (hint: use a regular expression).

2. Add a short description to the HTML interface of the DownloadRepeatRegion.htm file.

3. Create a new Server Behavior control for a text area based on the TextField control.

CHAPTER 6

The Dreamweaver Menus and Extension Packaging

IN THIS CHAPTER:

Packaging Extensions

Using Shared Files in Your Extension Package

Extension Organization

Adding Your Own Menu and Menu Items

Adding an Item to the Context Menus

Using the MXI File Creator Packager Extension

What to Take Away from this Chapter

Exercises

W e've covered the building of a few different extension types, but one of the areas of Dreamweaver that we've only briefly touched on is the menus.xml file. This file, along with other menu files, contains the entire menu structure of Dreamweaver. Inside this file you will find all of the menu information of Dreamweaver, including such things as the File, Edit, and View menus as well as all of the various contextual menus that make the Dreamweaver user's life easier. By having all of the menus and menu items in an XML file such as this, you are free to modify the menu structure of Dreamweaver to add new items if you want to. In other words, the menus can be extended, too.

The menus.xml File

We've mentioned that menus should not be edited directly, but if they are, they should be edited very carefully. How do you make changes to a menu without physically changing one? By using an extension *package*. Dreamweaver 4 comes with the Extension Manager that also includes a built-in packager for extensions. The Macromedia Extension Package format (MXP) is the extension package file format for Dreamweaver extensions created with the Extension Manager. The package can be created from files that make up an extension or it can be just a menu change by itself—menu writing and changing commands are part of the MXP file format. We'll outline the creation of a packageby directly packaging one of the extensions you created in Chapter 4.

Packaging Extensions

The package is created by first writing a Macromedia Extension Installation (MXI) file with all of the information about your extension. The MXI file is in a limited XML format. It's not *true* XML, but it's a subset that is recognized by the Dreamweaver API. To write your MXI file, you can use the template that's included in the Extension Manager folder, or you can modify an existing MXI file.

When you install a third-party extension, the MXI files are unpacked to the Extensions folder under Configuration. These files don't have an editor associated with them, but they can be opened from Notepad, BBEdit, or any text editor. Make sure you save the file as plain text after you make your changes to the file.

We'll go through the process of creating the MXI file and packaging an extension by using the Extension Mini Editor floater that was built in Chapter 4.

Main Tag

The main tag of the MXI file is the `<macromedia-extension>` tag. This tag specifies the name, version, type, and the optional attribute of "requires-restart." In addition, if you submit the extension to the Macromedia Exchange, MM will insert an ID number into this tag. The ID number should not be edited, however.

```
<macromedia-extension
   name="Extension Mini Editor"
   version="1.0.0"
   type="Floater"
   requires-restart="true" >
```

The name should be a unique name, usually the same as the title that you give to the extension in the HTML file of that extension. The version number consists of three digits in *major.minor.micro* format representing the main version number, the revision number, and the micro revision number. For example, if you begin with 1.0.0 and make a bug fix, you should number the next version 1.0.1, and so on. These are considered micro revisions, whereas a complete change in the interface or the functionality would be a major change that you would want to revise as a new version number, such as 2.0.0. The *type* attribute should be one of the extension types recognized by Dreamweaver. The *requires-restart* attribute is optional and should be used if your extension requires Dreamweaver to be restarted after the extension is installed. Most extensions require a restart, so it's always wise to include this line.

Products and Authors Tags

The next tag is the `<product>` tag, which consists of the names of the programs that the extension will work with. Some commands, objects, behaviors, and other extensions might work with Dreamweaver in addition to UltraDev, but extensions such as Server Behaviors and other server related extensions should be defined as UltraDev-only by specifying it in this tag. The tag allows the lowest common denominator to use the extension, so if you specify Dreamweaver 3, the extension will work in Dreamweaver 3 and 4 and UltraDev 1 and 4. In this case, you'll specify Dreamweaver 4:

```
<products>
    <product name="Dreamweaver" version="4" primary="true"/>
</products>
```

Next is the Author Name tag, which you can use to identify the extension as written by you, or you can put your company name here.

```
<author  name="Thomas Muck"> </author>
```

Description of the Extension

The next required tag is the description of the extension, using a `<description>` tag. Inside of this tag is a *CDATA* directive that sets off the start of your description data. CDATA allows the use of special characters (such as tags) within the XML tags. Everything within the CDATA brackets will be taken literally. The description should indicate the basic functionality and usage of the extension. The text of the description can contain HTML limited to `<br>` tags and * * characters:

```
<description>
<![CDATA[
By adding this floater to a web page, you can view, edit,
and reload extensions in the floater, as well as reload
menus and evaluate JavaScript snippets.
]]>
</description>
```

TIP

*If your extension description is complex, make liberal use of **
** and   in your description—spaces, tabs, and new lines are ignored when the description is displayed in the Extension Manager.*

After the description of the extension is the `<UI-Access>` tag, in which you describe how the extension is accessed and applied to the Web page. The `<UI-Access>` tag also has the CDATA directive and has the same HTML restrictions as the `<description>` tag:

```
<UI-Access>
<![CDATA[
Access this extension by choosing:<br>
Windows >> Extension Mini Editor]]>
</UI-Access>
```

Putting Your Files into the Extension Package

Before you package your extension, you should copy all of the files to a *staging area*, which can be a central folder for all of your extension packages, or it can be a folder that mimics the directory structure of the Dreamweaver Configuration folder.

Macromedia advises against packaging the extensions directly from within the Dreamweaver environment. You can try to keep a folder that has all of your extension packages in separate subfolders within a main extension package staging area.

The files are specified within the <files> tag. The child tag of the <files> tag is the <file> tag, where you actually give the names of each file that is to be included in the extension package. By keeping the MXI file within this same staging area folder, you can keep your packaging paths simple for the <file> tag.

```
<files>

<file name="Extension Mini Editor.htm"
 destination="$dreamweaver/Configuration/Floaters/">
</file>
<file name="smBD.gif"
 destination="$dreamweaver/Configuration/Shared/Basic-UltraDev/images"
 shared="true">
</file>
<file name="browsefolder.gif"
 destination="$dreamweaver/Configuration/Shared/Basic-UltraDev/images"
 shared="true">
</file>
<file name="duplicate.gif"
 destination="$dreamweaver/Configuration/Shared/Basic-UltraDev/images"
 shared="true">
</file>
<file name="new.gif"
 destination="$dreamweaver/Configuration/Shared/Basic-UltraDev/images"
 shared="true">
</file>
<file name="open.gif"
 destination="$dreamweaver/Configuration/Shared/Basic-UltraDev/images"
 shared="true">
</file>
<file name="save.gif"
 destination="$dreamweaver/Configuration/Shared/Basic-UltraDev/images"
 shared="true">
</file>
<file name="trash.gif"
 destination="$dreamweaver/Configuration/Shared/Basic-UltraDev/images"
 shared="true">
</file>
</files>
```

TIP

The filename always has to be a relative path to the file from the MXI file. By using a staging area, you can eliminate the complex use of paths in your filenames and simply name the file directly.

The filename is given and must be listed as a relative path to the MXI file. The destination is also given as a path, with the path referencing the Dreamweaver root folder by using a $dreamweaver directive. This is a built-in variable that refers to the program that is receiving the installation and is the same for both Dreamweaver and UltraDev. The other options at the present time are $ultradev, $flash, $fireworks, and $system, for the path to the system folder on the computer where the extension is being installed.

Changing the Dreamweaver Menus

Next are the configuration changes. This is where you make the additions to the various menus within Dreamweaver. In fact, you can build an extension that is nothing but menu changes. Say you wanted the Paste as Text command to be accessible from the contextual menu to conform to your work habits. You could edit the menus.xml file by hand, or you could create an MXI file with the menu change spelled out in a configuration-changes tag. This way, the changes can be undone simply by removing the extension from Dreamweaver. It's a better way to handle your menus so that the changes you make to the menu can be documented and undone if the need arises.

The configuration-changes tag for this particular extension is as follows:

```
<configuration-changes>
 <menu-insert appendTo="DWMenu_Window">
  <menuitem name="Extension Mini Editor"
    enabled="true"
    command="dw.toggleFloater('Extension Mini Editor')"
    checked="dw.getFloaterVisibility('Extension Mini Editor')"
    id="TFM_DWMenu_Window_ExtensionEditor" />
  </menu-insert>
</configuration-changes>
```

You'll notice the ID attribute that was added to the menu items. The ID should be something unique to your extension. Macromedia recommends adding a unique prefix to the beginning of the menu item. For instance, a menu item was added to the DWMenu_Window menu. By adding a prefix to the name and adding the extension name to the end of the ID, you've created a unique menu-item ID. This is necessary to avoid conflicts with other extensions written by yourself or other people.

If you include directives in the MXI file to explicitly add your extension to a menu, you can include the line `<!--MENU-LOCATION=NONE-->` as the first line in your extension to prevent Dreamweaver from looking at your extension when it starts up and builds the menus. It's not necessary to include this line, however.

Wrapping Up the Package

After completing all of the required tags, you must close out the main tag, which will complete the MXI file.

```
</macromedia-extension>
```

Now that you have an MXI file for the extension, you can open it up in the Macromedia Extension Manager by double-clicking the MXI file. The process is simple, and now you are prompted for Extension to Package, as shown in Figure 6-1, and the filename to "Save Package As," as shown in Figure 6-2. The packager itself doesn't have an interface other than this Open/Save dialog.

NOTE

The Extension Manager has to be closed in order for the packaging to take place by double-clicking the extension MXI file. If the Extension Manager is open when you double-click the MXI file, the Extension Manager will attempt to install the extension instead of packaging it. In fact, doing this allows you to install the extension without having to create a package file (MXP).

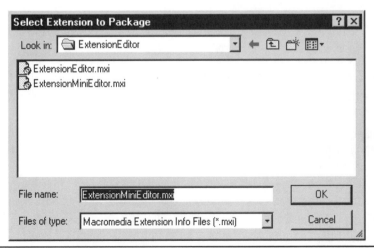

Figure 6-1   *Packaging an extension using the Extension Manager—first you are prompted for the MXI file*

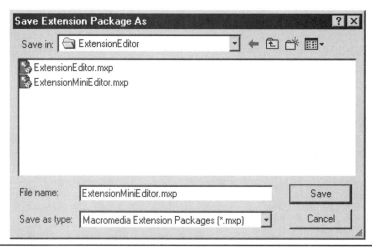

Figure 6-2 *Next you are prompted for the name of the package to create*

After this process is completed, you can install the extension in any machine by using the MXP file that is the result of the packaging operation. The MXP file contains all of the files of your extension, as well as the MXI file to tell Dreamweaver where to put the files and what changes to make to the Dreamweaver menus. When the extension is installed, the MXI file is installed to the Extensions folder under Configuration so that the Extension Manager can keep track of which extensions are installed.

TIP

It's always a good idea to keep a clean Configuration folder so you can switch it in and out to test extension packages on a fresh installation of Dreamweaver.

Inside the Extension Manager is the option to "turn off" the extension by unchecking the box in the On/Off column in the Extension Manager interface, as shown in Figure 6-3. Behind the scenes, this removes all of the files from the folders, repackages them, and removes any changes that were made to the menus. In effect, the extension is uninstalled, but the entry remains in the Extension Manager so that the extension can be reactivated by checking the On/Off box once again. The extension is then reinstalled by the Extension Manager.

Packaged extensions can be submitted to the Macromedia Exchange and shared with other users. The submission process is outlined on the Macromedia Exchange Web site. Macromedia quality assurance (QA) engineers test the extension when you upload it. It's a good indication that the extension is safe to install if it appears on the Exchange. In addition to the submission, there is also an option for a Macromedia seal of approval, which means that the extension has been tested for user interface

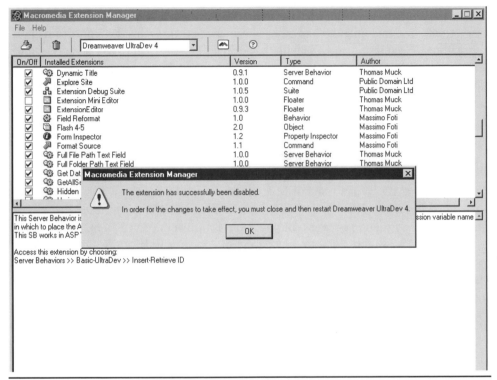

Figure 6-3   *You can turn off extensions with a check box in the Extension Manager*

and compatibility issues using stricter guidelines by the Macromedia QA engineers. Whether you choose to do this or not, extensions should be packaged to make it easier to keep track of changes to your menus and configuration files, in addition to the ease of removing the installed extensions, and transporting extensions.

Using Shared Files in Your Extension Package

One of the things that you may have noticed about the `<file>` tags in the Extension Mini Editor extension that you just packaged is that there are some shared image files contained in the package, as in this tag:

```
<file name="open.gif"
 destination="$dreamweaver/Configuration/Shared/Basic-UltraDev/images"
 shared="true">
</file>
```

By using the *shared* attribute and setting it to *true*, the file in question is written to the user's Configuration folder. Unlike other files in the extension that are uninstalled upon uninstalling the extension, any file with the attribute *shared="true"* will be left behind, if other extensions need it. This is because the file can be shared between different extensions. For example, suppose you wrote another extension that had an Open File button and you needed to use the same open.gif icon in the extension. You certainly don't want two copies of the file existing simultaneously; you also don't want the file to be uninstalled upon uninstalling the extension. The shared attribute takes care of this.

Images aren't the only files that can be shared—scripts contained in .js files are also often shared among extensions. One of the things that we mentioned early in this book is that if you use some of Macromedia's shared functions in your extension it is sometimes a good idea to put a copy of the file into your own shared library file. This way, if the function is ever removed from future versions of Dreamweaver, you won't run the risk of having your extension fail. One example of this that comes to mind is our own Pages List Server Behavior that used a shared common file that was in UltraDev 1. When UltraDev 4 came out, the file was changed and most of the functionality was placed into XML files and removed from the .js file. This caused the Pages List extension to fail with the new version of UltraDev.

One possible side effect of having shared functions is that you may have a newer version of a function in your extensions some day. There is no version control in the shared files in the latest version of the Extension Manager as of this writing (version 1.2), so if your newer extension overwrites the old file with a new version of the file, the old extension could possibly stop working. Another possibility is that an older file that is installed afterwards could overwrite your newer file. These are all things to consider when you are updating shared files.

Many of the great features of Dreamweaver are contained in the Shared directory in the MM folder. Appendix A lists a few of these functions. In addition, you can find a wealth of information in the Shared directory under the folders of other developers whose extensions you've installed. Keep in mind when you use files or functions written by other people that the original author is usually the sole owner of the code. While many extension developers freely share this code, it's always wise to obtain permission from the author if you plan to use the code.

Extension Organization

When you add an extension to Dreamweaver but don't explicitly write out the menu location, the menu item is frequently appended to the bottom of the list in the menu. For example, if you add objects to the Objects folder, the Insert menu starts to get a little long and hard to read. The same thing is true of the Commands menu, Server Behaviors menu, and any other menu that gets its content from the various Configuration folders.

One way that developers have come up with to ease the organizational headache is to place extensions that they've written into their own subfolder and corresponding menu item. For example, our extensions are generally listed in the Basic-UltraDev menu whenever possible. However, this can frequently get out of hand as well, once you start to develop many extensions. There really isn't a hard-and-fast rule for organizing menus; you should use your own judgment when creating your extensions. For example, if you are creating a set of Behaviors that deal with your own tag system, you should organize the extensions into their own menu and further subdivide the menu into other menus if it becomes cumbersome. Objects and commands have slightly different menu structures and only allow one layer of nested directories, as in Objects | MyFolder, whereas in Behaviors and Server Behaviors you can nest your directories.

Another way to help the organization of your extensions within the menu system is to use menu item dividers frequently. You can insert a menu item divider directly into the menu or you can code it into the MXI file between `<menu-item>` tags when you package an extension, like this:

```
<menu-insert appendTo="DWMenu_Window">
<separator id="TFM_DWMenu_Window_ExtensionEditor_SeparatorBefore" />
<menuitem name="Extension Mini Editor"
    enabled="true"
    command="dw.toggleFloater('Extension Mini Editor')"
    checked="dw.getFloaterVisibility('Extension Mini Editor')"
    domRequired="false"
    id="TFM_DWMenu_Window_ExtensionEditor" />
</menu-insert>
```

We've given the menu item separator an *ID* attribute just like a menu item and given it a descriptive name so that we can later reference it if we want. For example, we could later add a menu item directly above or below this separator by referencing the ID when we write a `<menu-insert>` tag.

Adding Your Own Menu and Menu Items

After creating an extension package and making your own menu items, you might begin to think that it should be possible to create your own menus in addition to menu items. You can. In Dreamweaver, you aren't limited to the menus that you see—you can easily create your own. Let's create a new menu for accessing your own personal Web sites or tutorials so that they are always within reach. One possible use of such a system is to set up a frequently used page, such as a Login page, as a menu item so that you can test out the site by logging in easily.

Start by deciding what to put in the menu and where to put it. Since there is plenty of room after the standard Help menu on the menu bar, put the new menu right before the Help menu and push the Help menu over. It could easily fit between other menus if you prefer. The menu will be called MySites and it will have four menu items to start with: the Basic-UltraDev site, for the fine extensions and tutorials that you can find there; Massimo's corner of the Web, for its great extensions; the Configuration folder; and a page in the current site. For UltraDev, this is especially handy if you have a central Login page that is the entry point for your application. If you have page-level protection on the current page, you might want to preview the page by logging in and browsing to that page.

Here are the menu entries that need to be made:

```
<menu name="MySites" id="TFM_DWMenu_MySites">
  <menuitem name="Basic-UltraDev" enabled="true"
   command="dw.browseDocument('http://www.basic-ultradev.com')"
   id="TFM_DWMenu_MySites_BUD1" />
  <menuitem name="Massimo's Corner" enabled="true"
   command="dw.browseDocument('http://www.massimocorner.com')"
   id="TFM_DWMenu_MySites_BUD2" />
  <menuitem name="Configuration" enabled="true"
   command="dw.browseDocument(dw.getConfigurationPath())"
   id="TFM_DWMenu_MySites_BUD3" />
  <menuitem name="This site default" enabled="true"
   command="dw.browseDocument('http://localhost/home.asp')"
```

```
      id="TFM_DWMenu_MySites_BUD4" />
</menu>
```

This would be quite easy to code by hand directly into the menu. You could simply cut and paste the code into the menus.xml file. Two months from now after a reinstall, though, you'll have forgotten what you did to the menu, and there won't be an easy way to recover your changes.

That's where the MXP file comes in. You're not "packaging" an extension per se—there are no files to package. The only things that are going into the file are the menu changes. These can then be installed and uninstalled at will.

Here is the code for the MXI file. The only thing that you're doing differently from the Extension Mini Editor package that you created earlier is that there are no files included:

```
<macromedia-package
   name="MySites"
   version="1.0.0"|
   type="command"
   requires-restart="true">
<author name="Thomas Muck" />
<products>
   <product name="Dreamweaver" version="4" />
</products>
<description>
   <![CDATA[
      Add a list of sites to a new menu called MySites
   ]]>
</description>
<ui-access>
   <![CDATA[
      The new menu MySites will be accessible from the
      standard menu bar.|
   ]]>
</ui-access>
<configuration-changes>
  <menu-insert insertBefore="DWMenu_Help">
    <menu name="MySites" enabled="true"
     id="TFM_DWMenu_MySites" />
  </menu-insert>
  <menu-insert appendTo="TFM_DWMenu_MySites">
```

```
    <menuitem name="Basic-UltraDev"
     enabled="true"
     command="dw.browseDocument('http://www.basic-ultradev.com')"
     id="TFM_DWMenu_MySites_BUD1" />
  </menu-insert>
  <menu-insert appendTo="TFM_DWMenu_MySites">
    <menuitem name="Massimo's Corner"
     enabled="true"
     command="dw.browseDocument('http://www.massimocorner.com')"
     id="TFM_DWMenu_MySites_BUD2" />
  </menu-insert>
  <menu-insert appendTo="TFM_DWMenu_MySites">
    <menuitem name="This site default"
     enabled="true"
     command="dw.browseDocument('http://localhost/home.asp')"
     id="TFM_DWMenu_MySites_BUD4" />
  </menu-insert>
  <menu-insert appendTo="TFM_DWMenu_MySites">
    <separator id="TFM_DWMenu_MySites_Separator" />
    <menuitem name="Configuration"
     enabled="true"
     command="dw.browseDocument(dw.getConfigurationPath())"
     id="TFM_DWMenu_MySites_BUD3" />
  </menu-insert>
</configuration-changes>
</macromedia-package>
```

After defining the package, products, author, and description, add the menu and the menu items. The first <menu-insert> tag has a directive of insertBefore="DWMenu_Help". You specified the DWMenu_Help menu, so the menu will be inserted directly in front of the Help menu. The other possible directives are insertAfter, appendTo, and prependTo. Using this <menu-insert> tag, you inserted the new menu with a <menu> tag. The *ID* attribute of the <menu> tag will later be used by the other <menu-insert> tags so that the new menu items will be appended to the new menu. This is the primary reason for *ID* attributes and the reason no two IDs should be the same—if you had two the same, you would never be able to reference the second one.

If you package and install this extension now, you will see a new menu next to the Help menu that lists the four items that you added, shown in Figure 6-4. You can add more items the same way if you want to so that the menu is truly useful for you.

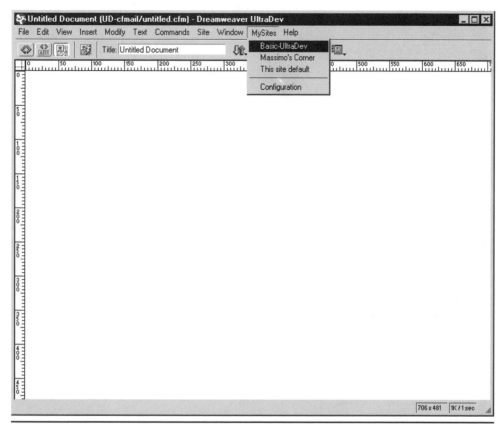

Figure 6-4   *The new menu and menu items that you just added*

Adding an Item to the Context Menus

The contextual menus in Dreamweaver are many. When you are on a blank page, there is one context menu. If you are in a table cell, there is another. If you are inside a layer, there is yet another. There are context menus for almost every facet of Dreamweaver. Context menus are probably the best place to put your most often-used commands. How often have you right-clicked and copied and pasted something from one spot to another or one page to the next? On a Macintosh the context menus are not quite as handy, since you have to hold down the CONTROL key while you click, but on a Windows system the contextual menus make life really easy for the user.

Adding an item to the contextual menu is just as easy as adding a menu item to any other menu. There is one thing that you have to be aware of though: if you want your item to be available to you in the design environment, it has to be placed into each context menu where it may apply. For example, a Copy/Paste command seems to be available from the context menu wherever you happen to be. The fact of the matter is that the copy and paste commands are listed in over 20 different menus. This can be quite cumbersome when you want to add an often-used command to a menu—which menus do you put it in?

There is no hard-and-fast rule, but your general page editing functions can be done in four different locations, and menu items should be placed in all four of these contextual menus to be really useful. You could be inside a blank page, in which case you would use the DWTextContext menu. Or you could be in a table cell, in which case you would use the DWContext_Table menu. If you were inside a layer or div, you would want the item to be placed in the DWContext_Layer menu. Lastly, if you were in Code view, you would want the item placed in the DWContext_HTML menu. That's four locations for starters. The following code is from our QuickLink command, which inserts a link maker into each of the four contextual menus:

```
<configuration-changes>
<menu-insert appendTo="DWContext_Text">
  <menuitem name="QuickLink"
   enabled="true" file="Commands/QuickLink.htm"
   id="TFM_DWContext_Text_QuickLink" />
</menu-insert>
<menu-insert appendTo="DWContext_Layer">
  <menuitem name="QuickLink" enabled="true"
   file="Commands/QuickLink.htm"
   id="TFM_DWContext_Layer_QuickLink" />
</menu-insert>
<menu-insert appendTo="DWContext_HTML">
  <menuitem name="QuickLink" enabled="true"
   file="Commands/QuickLink.htm"
   id="TFM_DWContext_HTML_QuickLink" />
</menu-insert>
<menu-insert appendTo="DWContext_Table">
  <menuitem name="QuickLink" enabled="true"
   file="Commands/QuickLink.htm"
   id="TFM_DWContext_Table_QuickLink" />
</menu-insert>
</configuration-changes>
```

The only thing that these MXI `<menu-insert>` tags are doing is inserting a menu item reference to the same command file in four different contextual menus. The effect of doing this is that the QuickLink command is now within reach via right-click anywhere you are on the page, whether you are on a blank page, in a table cell, inside a layer, or in Code view.

You can also put commands right into a contextual menu. This was shown earlier with a regular menu and is quite handy for a contextual menu. The following line will add a menu command that will be in the form element contextual menu and prompt the user for a *tabindex* attribute.

```
<menu-insert appendTo="DWFormFieldContext">
<menuitem name="Change the Tabindex" enabled="true"
  command="dw.getDocumentDOM().getSelectedNode().setAttribute(
  'tabindex',prompt('Change the Tabindex'));"
  id="TFM_DWFormFieldContext_Tabindex" />
</menu-insert>
```

By putting the call to the `setAttribute()` method of the `getSelectedNode()` method of the DOM, you are effectively creating a command within the menu itself, as you've already seen. What is different here, though, is the fact that the command will only come into play when a form field is selected (except for a list box and button— they have different context menus, but they can also be changed easily). The user will be prompted for a *tabindex* attribute and the attribute will be set after clicking OK.

One thing this command doesn't do is to supply the current *tabindex* attribute to the user. You can add that by adding a default value to the JavaScript prompt box that was used in the previous example, like this:

```
prompt('Change the Tabindex',
dw.getDocumentDOM().getSelectedNode().getAttribute('tabindex'))
```

Now all you have to do is wrap it up into an MXI file, and the extension is finished:

```
<macromedia-package
  name="Add Tabindex Attribute"
  version="1.0.0"
  type="command"
  requires-restart="true">
  <author name="Thomas Muck" />
  <products>
```

```
    <product name="Dreamweaver" version="4" primary="true"/>
    <product name="UltraDev" version="4" />
  </products>
  <description>
  <![CDATA[
    Adds a new menu item to the form field contextual menu
    to prompt the user for a tabindex attribute
  ]]>
  </description>
  <ui-access>
  <![CDATA[
    Accessible from the form field contextual menu.
  ]]>
  </ui-access>
  <configuration-changes>
    <menu-insert appendTo="DWFormFieldContext">
    <menuitem name="Change the Tabindex" enabled="true"
command="dw.getDocumentDOM().getSelectedNode().setAttribute(
'tabindex',prompt('Change the Tabindex',
dw.getDocumentDOM().getSelectedNode().getAttribute('tabindex')));"
id="TFM_DWFormFieldContext_Tabindex" />
    </menu-insert>
  </configuration-changes>
</macromedia-package>
```

After creating this MXI file in Notepad, BBEdit, or your text editor of choice, you can make the package and use the package to update your menu.

CAUTION

*There is a bug in the Extension Manager version 1.2 that can cause problems when installing extensions. It is always wise to make fresh backups of your menus.xml file frequently, especially because this bug has no reproducible steps. There is a technote at **www.macromedia.com/ support/dreamweaver/ts/documents/em_menus_xbk.htm**. We're hoping that the bug will be fixed by the time this book is released.*

Using the MXI File Creator Packager Extension

There is an easier way to package extensions than creating them manually using a text editor, and that is with the MXI File Creator Packager Extension. Public Domain Ltd., a company that specializes in custom extensions for Dreamweaver, created this extension. It is available freely on the Macromedia Exchange, and it is the method of choice for many people for packaging extensions. Although using this extension speeds up the MXI file creation process, it is still important to know the underlying MXI file structure.

To use this extension, you have to first download and install it from the Macromedia Exchange. There have been several versions of the extension, but the current one as of the writing of this book is version 1.6.1. Public Domain is always pushing the limits of Dreamweaver extension creation, and this extension is no exception.

The command is located in the Commands menu and is called Public Domain MXI File Creator. When you first start up the extension, you'll have to fill in a few default values, such as the author name. These preferences are saved in an XML file in the PublicDomain shared folder and will be used each time you start up the extension. The interface is shown in Figure 6-5.

The interface has seven tabs, and you can move back and forth between tabs to add your data to the MXI file. The buttons on the right allow you to save the package as a Project file with an .xpf file extension. This allows you to create reusable package projects so that you can go back to the original package when you make

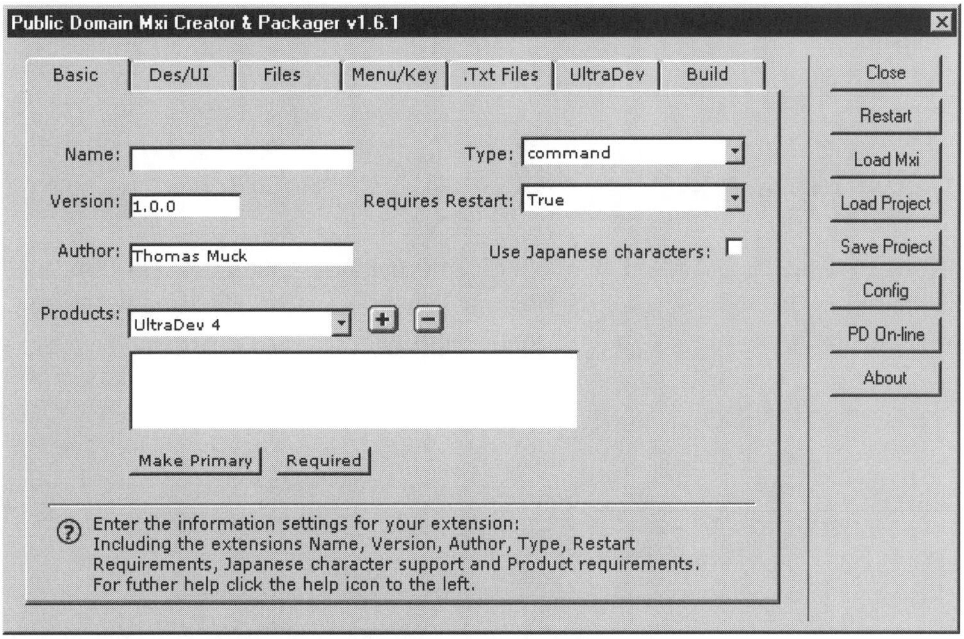

Figure 6-5   *The Public Domain MXI File Creator*

changes. Also, there is a button for Load MXI that allows you to load an existing MXI file and turn it into a Public Domain MXI File Creator project.

The first tab contains the basic information, such as the extension name, author, and the products that the extension will work with. You can choose products and add them to the list and then pick a primary product, such as Dreamweaver 3. Also, this is where you set the extension type from a drop-down list of all available extension types.

The second tab is where you put the Description and UI Access information, as shown here:

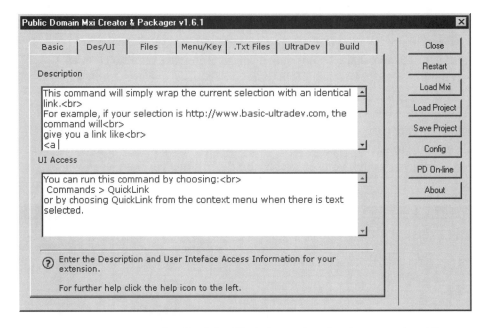

Tab 3 is where you can add all of the file information for the extension. The buttons allow you to browse for the files and then browse to the location where you want the files to be installed to. First you click Add File:

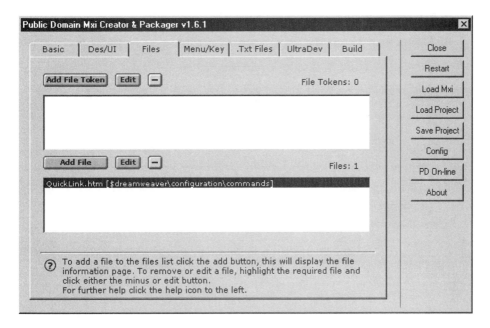

That brings up another dialog in the same tab that allows you to pick the file and destination folder. You can also set the Shared attribute and platform from this tab:

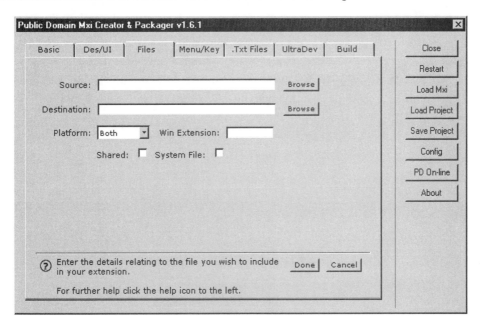

The fourth tab allows you to add menus and menu items. These are the same menu items that were outlined earlier, but the MXI File Creator makes the process much easier.

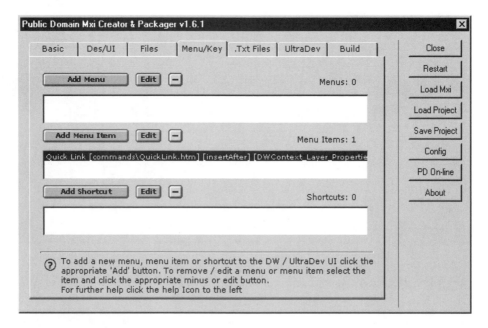

Simply add your menus and menu items to the box, and the tags are automatically written for you. The menus and menu items are loaded into drop-down boxes so that you can easily find the menu that you want to insert your item into. These drop-downs are loaded directly from the live menus.xml file, so that if any custom menu items already exist, they will show up in the drop-down box:

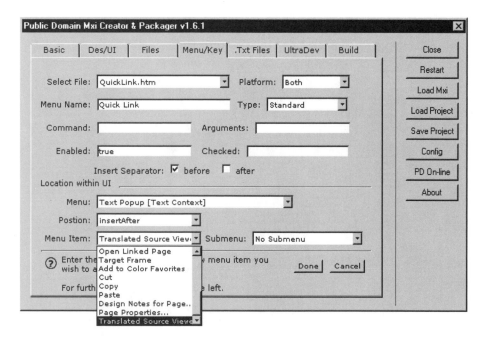

Tab 5 allows you to change some of the text files that are customizable in Dreamweaver, like the Extensions.txt file and the FTPExtensions.txt file:

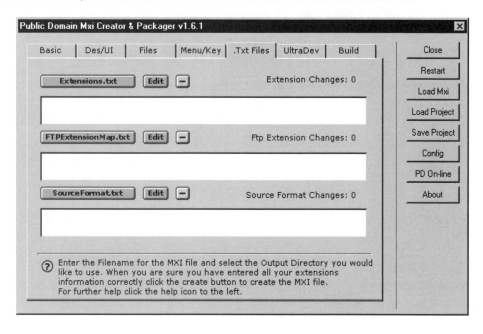

If you're ever in doubt about what to do in the MXI File Creator, the question mark (?) icon in the bottom left-hand corner of the extension has contextual help available for most topics within the extension, shown here for tab 6:

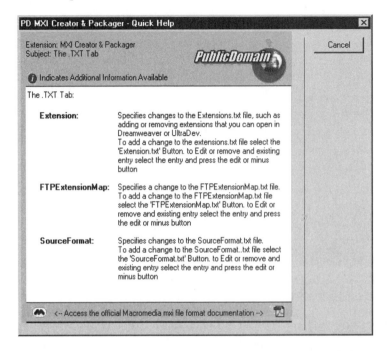

The sixth tab allows you to directly type in any UltraDev-specific tags:

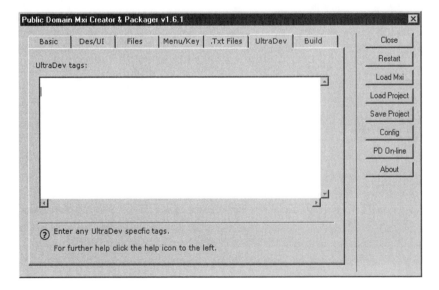

Finally, the seventh and last tab allows you to create the actual package for the extension. The tab also has buttons to launch the Extension Manager and to submit the package to the Macromedia Exchange.

The Public Domain MXI File Creator is one of the best extensions on the Exchange, and it's one that you can use to your advantage as an extension writer.

What to Take Away from this Chapter

This chapter introduced the MXI file format and menu editing from the MXI file. The MXI file format is the standard Dreamweaver extension package format, and it should be learned as part of the extension building process. Shared files were discussed as well, since they are a big part of the extension package. Extension organization was discussed in the context of packaging, since the extension package will determine where your extensions are installed and accessed from. Finally, a shortcut to building the MXI files was shown in the form of the Public Domain MXI File Creator Packager, which can automate the process of extension packaging.

Exercises

1. Create an extension package for the Car object created in Chapter 2 and be sure to include the Car Inspector that you built as an exercise in Chapter 4.

2. Create an extension package using the Public Domain MXI File Creator Packager that adds a Paste As Text menu item to the HTML code view window. Hint: find the appropriate API call in the documentation and include it directly in the <menu-item> tag.

3. Come up with three new items that would make good choices for contextual menu items and implement them with an extension package.

Testing and Deploying Extensions

IN THIS CHAPTER:

W e covered several of the more popular extension types in the first six chapters. Extension writing at its core is the means to an end: making the production environment more productive. As a Dreamweaver extension writer, you can do that by bolting more functionality onto the core program. The final extension should speed up or make easier the whole process of Web programming and Web design in the Dreamweaver environment. Using the proper techniques and tools while constructing extensions can also speed up the extension writing process.

Testing and Debugging the Extension

Testing extensions is never easy, as there really isn't a dedicated environment for debugging and editing the extension. You can use your own text editor of choice, or you can even edit the files in Dreamweaver itself. One of the drawbacks to using Dreamweaver or UltraDev for editing your extension is that you have to have your site set up in the Configuration folder. While this might not be a huge burden if you are using Dreamweaver, it may be problematic while testing UltraDev extensions, since it's really possible to set up a server model for the Configuration folder or test any server-side code.

The other drawback is the fact that your extension probably performs some sort of action or inserts some code on a page, and you want to be able to test that extension on a real page to see what does and doesn't work. This is easily done by having Dreamweaver open in a regular site and editing your extension in another environment, such as Homesite or BBEdit. You could even use the Extension Mini Editor that was created in Chapter 4, which has the handy Reload Extensions and Reload Menus buttons built right into the interface. This would allow you to load your extension, edit it, save it, and reload extensions from one interface.

Extensions should be tested for bugs, and the code that you are inserting in the page should be tested as well. Sometimes it's not easy to test on all the different platforms and browsers that your code will be running on. That's when the user groups come in handy. There are groups dedicated to extension writing and testing, and you should locate one and become a member. In addition, there are discussion boards dedicated to Dreamweaver, including Macromedia's forums at **news:// forums.macromedia.com**, where you can post a link to your extension; people will then test it for you and report any problems that they may have. What may work on your computer on Internet Explorer and Netscape may not work on someone else's computer that has a different configuration or different version of the browser.

Whichever method you choose, you'll need some way to test the variables, objects, and functions that make up your extensions. We'll show some of the methods available to the extension writer.

Using Alert Boxes

Alert boxes are built into JavaScript as a way to display information to the user, with a simple OK button on the box to close it down. It is also the prime method for debugging JavaScript—inside client-side code on a Web page or in a Dreamweaver extension.

One way to use alert boxes is to place them in key positions within your extension. For example, if you are trying to determine whether a part of your script is working properly, you can place alert boxes that display variables in your extension file. As an example, look at this code from the CommentCommands file in Chapter 3:

```
function makeComment() {
// Get Selected text and wrap with comment tags
    var dom = dw.getDocumentDOM();//get the dom
    var sel = dom.getSelection();//get the selected text or object
alert(sel);
    var wrapthis = dom.documentElement.outerHTML.substring(sel[0], sel[1]);
alert(wrapthis);
    wrapthis = openTag + wrapthis + closeTag;//wrap the selected text
alert(wrapthis);
    dw.getDocumentDOM().insertHTML(wrapthis);//insert into the document
    window.close();
}
```

We've inserted three alert boxes to show the values of the variables *sel*, *wrapthis* before concatenating the string, and *wrapthis* after concatenating the string. After changing the code and inserting the alert boxes, you have to save the file and either restart Dreamweaver or reload the extensions. Then you can select some text or object on a page and apply the command. Three alert boxes should pop up, one after the other. The first one will look something like this:

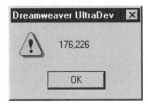

In the alert box should be the result of the first variable, *sel*. This variable happens to contain two values in an array, which will display in the alert box as two comma-separated numerical values—the beginning and ending offsets into the document of the current selection. The next alert box will contain the actual selection.

In this particular instance, we've highlighted an image on the page and selected it. If you count the characters in the alert box, it should be equal to the difference of the offsets in the first alert box. The next alert box should contain the selection after applying the comment tags around it.

If all three alert boxes contain the information you are expecting, then the function is probably working right.

You can also use alert boxes to display the result of a called function, if that function has a return value. For example, if you are calling a function named `getFilename()` that is supposed to return a variable that contains a filename, you can put an alert box in a position where you would be calling the function from, like this:

```
alert(getFilename())
```

The function `getFilename` will be evaluated before the alert box is fired because parentheses are always evaluated from the inside out. The result will be that you'll see whether the function is returning the proper value.

You can test out arrays in this way as well. Take a look at this function from an UltraDev Server Behavior. We've placed an alert box in a key place within a loop so that each element of the array will be displayed in the alert box:

```
function findServerBehaviors(){
  var i, ssRec, ssRecList = new Array();
  var dom = dw.getDocumentDOM();
```

```
  var nodes = findLockedScriptNodes(dom);
  for (i=0; i<nodes.length; i++) {
alert(unescape(nodes[i].orig))
    tagStr=unescape(nodes[i].orig);
    if (tagStr.match(getServerData("prep","myServerBehavior"))) {
      ssRec = buildSSRecord(nodes[i]);
      if (ssRec) ssRecList.push(ssRec); //add record to the array
    }
  }
```

In this case, you will display the code from every server-side code block on
the page. This way, you'll make sure that you are retrieving the correct information.
Do you want translated or untranslated values? The alert box will show you exactly
what is being retrieved. Later, you can put an alert box inside of the *if* statement to
see if the match is ever executed. If you're ever in doubt as to whether your code is
being executed, use an alert box.

When you're developing a substantial extension that will require more testing
than usual, you can hard-code alert boxes right into the extension and turn them on
and off with a debug switch. This will be a Boolean variable that is set to true or
false depending on whether you are in debug mode or not. When we say "debug
mode," we are referring to a state in the extension that you set up yourself by setting
the Boolean value to true, as in the following example. First, set up the debug mode
by setting our switch on:

```
var TFM_debug = true;
//var TFM_debug = false;
```

Notice that there is a false and a true value, and one of them is commented out.
This is the switch we were referring to—comment out the true value if you want to
turn debugging off, and comment out the false value to turn debugging on. Then,
inside of your code, you can do something like this:

```
if(TFM_debug) {
    alert("ssRec.rsname = " + ssRec.rsname + "\n" +
    "ssRec.columnname = " + ssRec.columnname + "\n" +
    "node.outerHTML = " + node.outerHTML)
}
```

If you sprinkle your code listing with debug statements like this, you can switch
debugging on and off easily and test the values of various variables, objects, and
functions from different places in your code. This is certainly easier than manually

inserting alerts when you want to test new conditions, especially when dealing with a complex extension that requires a lot of testing.

Using Eval and Trace Console

If you visit the Macromedia Exchange, you can download the Dreamweaver Platform SDK, which consists of several extensions to make debugging and testing extensions easier. One of these is Eval, which is a simple JavaScript evaluation command similar to the JavaScript evaluation we performed with the Extension Mini Editor in Chapter 4. It's accessible from the Commands menu and allows you to test values or expressions in JavaScript. One advantage it has over the floater is that it retains its value after closing the program down and restarting it, for debugging between sessions. You could easily adapt the command and create your own floater to perform a similar function.

Trace Console, on the other hand, is a complex extension that allows you to evaluate and trace variables, objects, and other extension information in a floater or have the output sent to a file. You can use it in place of alert boxes for complex interaction with your extension. Joe Marini, one of the primary developers on the Dreamweaver team, wrote Trace Console years ago, but it has only recently been in wide release, courtesy of the Macromedia Exchange. Figure 7-1 shows Trace Console examining the properties of an ssRecord object in a Server Behavior in UltraDev. Anyone who has developed Server Behaviors with UltraDev knows that the ssRecord object is a complex object with many properties and methods. Trace Console allows you to examine these easily.

To use Trace Console and Eval, along with other extension tools, you have to download and install the Dreamweaver Platform SDK (software development kit) from the Macromedia Exchange at **http://www.macromedia.com/exchange** and install it to your machine. The SDK will install all of the files needed into the SDK folder at the root of your Dreamweaver folder and also install the extensions into the appropriate locations in the Configuration folder.

The TraceConsole.js file contains all of the functionality of Trace Console. The actual console on which you will see the results of your debugging is the TraceConsole.htm file located in the Floaters folder. As your code is executed and the program comes across a method of Trace Console, the floater automatically pops up displaying the results of the method. To use it, you have to place an include line in the extension you are debugging (using the correct relative path), like this:

```
<script src="../Shared/MM/Scripts/TraceConsole.js"></script>
```

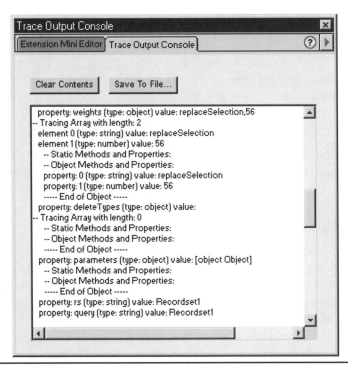

Figure 7-1   *Trace Console in the UltraDev environment examining the properties of an ssRecord object*

After including this line, you are free to use the methods of the Trace Console extension to debug your own extension. These methods are as follows:

▶ **traceString(str, bLineBreak)**   Sends a string to the console, with an optional line break after the string.

▶ **traceValues(bLineBreak, [param1,param2,...])**   Sends a list of variables or values to the console with an optional line break.

▶ **traceArray(aTheArray, bLineBreak, bIncludeLength, bIncludeElemTypes, bRecursiveTrace)**   Sends the contents of an array to the console. The optional parameters are for a line break, whether to include the length of the array, the element types, and whether to recursively trace objects of the array.

▶ **traceObject(oTheObj, bIncludeElemTypes, bIncludeStaticProps, bRecursiveTrace, [cIndentLevel])**   Sends an object to the console, with optional parameters for whether to include the types of the elements, the static class properties and methods, whether to recursively trace through properties of the object that are objects themselves, and an optional indentation level for the output text.

▶ **traceNode(oTheNode, bShowType, bShowContent, bShowParent, bShowChildCount)**   Traces a node of the DOM and displays properties and data of that node. The optional parameters are for whether to show the type of the node, the content, the parent, and the child count of the node.

▶ **traceCallChain(bIncludeArguments)**   Traces the entire chain of function calls up to the place where the traceCallChain method was called from. The only parameter is whether to include the arguments of the function calls in the Trace Console window or the output file.

▶ **clearTrace()**   Clears the window or text file.

There are other methods, most of which relate to the physical properties of the trace window or the debugging session, but the methods listed are the most frequently used during a debugging session. Consult the documentation that comes with the Dreamweaver Platform SDK for descriptions of the other methods.

The best way to show you the use of the console is to use it to examine one of the extensions that we built in Chapter 4—the Extension Mini Editor floater. You'll find that you can even use the Extension Mini Editor in conjunction with Trace Console by docking the two windows together.

Let's do a simple test of some values that are available in the resize function, setTextSize(). The function looks like this:

```
function setTextSize(a){
    if(a) window.resizeTo(500,400);
    var winWidth;
    var styleStr;
    if(dreamweaver.getFloaterVisibility("Extension Mini Editor")){
        winWidth = window.innerWidth;
        winHeight = window.innerHeight;
        styleStr = "width:" + (winWidth - 150) + "px";
        findObject('jsEvaluate').style = styleStr;
        styleStr = styleStr + "; height:" + (winHeight - 160) + "px";
        findObject('theCode').style = styleStr;
    }
}
```

Add this line to the end of the function before the closing brace:

```
traceValues(true, winWidth, winHeight, styleStr, a, theFile)
```

The `traceValues()` method is the simplest and most direct form of debugging—it will display a list of values that is passed to the function. In this case, you're passing it an argument of true to turn on the line break. The next four arguments are the variables used in the `setTextSize( )` function (`winWidth`, `winHeight`, `styleStr`, `a`). Finally, the last argument is a global variable that contains a filename (*theFile*). When you resize the window, the Trace Window is invoked and the variable values are displayed in the window:

```
traceValues: Tracing 6 arguments:

[553] [419] [width:403px; height:259px] [undefined] [file:///C|/Program
Files/Macromedia/Dreamweaver UltraDev 4/Configuration/Floaters/Extension
Mini Editor.htm]
```

You can see that tracing the variable values can make it easy to do the types of calculations necessary for the resize function of the window. Each time the window is resized, the new values are written to the Trace Window. Also, having all the values in one window in real-time is more convenient than using JavaScript alert boxes and clicking OK for each value that is displayed.

Using the same technique shown with alert boxes, you can have a global variable set up in the beginning of your file to turn debugging on and then call your Trace Console functions from within a debug code block, like this:

```
var TFM_debug = true;
//var TFM_debug = false;
//blah blah more code
if(TFM_debug) {
    traceString("My ssRecord Object called from
        inspectServerBehavior",true);
    traceObject(ssRec,true,true,true,true);
}
```

Trace Console might seem a little overwhelming at first, but after you get the hang of it you'll find yourself using it all the time.

The Public Domain Extension Debugger Extension

Another tool available for the extension developer was created by Public Domain—the Extension Debugger. This tool is for Windows only and allows you to edit and debug extensions in the Dreamweaver environment. After you install it, the right-click menu in Code view will be enabled with all of the methods available for debugging with the debugger. The following menu items are available for the debugger:

- ▶ **Start PD Debug Viewer**   Opens the Debug window. The debug window has a switch that will allow it to remain on top during your debugging session.

- ▶ **Close PD Debug Viewer**   Closes the Debug window.

- ▶ **Debug Selection**   Inserts a Debug.print() command into the file at the insertion point that evaluates the current selection into the preceding line within the active document.

- ▶ **Insert Debug Comment**   Inserts a Debug.comment() into the file on the next line.

- ▶ **Insert Debug Start**   Inserts a Debug.start() call at the current insertion point.

- ▶ **Insert Debug Stop**   Inserts a Debug.stop.

- ▶ **Insert Debug Pause**   Inserts a Debug.pause.

- ▶ **Insert Debug Clear**   Inserts a Debug.clear().

- ▶ **Remove Debug Code**   Removes all debug code from the currently active document. This command, in effect, ends the debugging session by allowing the document to revert to its original form.

- ▶ **Comment Debug Code**   Comments out any debug code with the currently active document.

- ▶ **Uncomment Debug Code**   Uncomments any debug code commented out within currently active document.

The Extensions Debugger comes with a PDF document that describes the functionality of the extension.

Repackaging and Version Control for Extensions

Version control (*versioning*) in Dreamweaver is taken care of by the extension developer, but it should follow the guidelines set forth by Macromedia. The numbering system is major.minor.micro and is used by the Extension Manager when it is installing an extension. Even if you have no plans to release the extensions, you should maintain strict version control for your own use. The Extension Manager will inform you when you are installing an older version or a newer version of the same extension.

The first version of your extension will be 1.0.0. Any test versions that are packaged before you have put the final nail in the project should be numbered as a zero version number, starting off with 0.1.0 and moving up until the final release version of 1.0.0. Any minor bug fixes should be noted by changing the micro number, as in 1.0.1. When you make a significant change in the functionality of the extension, you should increase the minor number (middle number), as in 1.1.0. Finally, when there are significant enough changes to warrant a new version number, you can increment the major number (first number) as in 2.0.0.

By maintaining strict version control of your extension, you will be able to tell whether you are running the most current version. More importantly, when releasing your extensions for public consumption, you'll be able to maintain the quality control on your extensions by addressing bugs when they arise and fixing them with new version numbers. If bugs are reported, you'll be able to quickly discover whether you've already addressed the problem and direct your user to a newer version of your extension.

When creating your extensions, it is best to keep them in a central packaging location or *staging area*. By doing this, it is easier to keep track of the changes you've made and all the files included in your extension. Generally, it is wise to keep backup copies of your extension staging areas and name the folders so that you can keep track of the different versions of your extensions. When creating a new version of an existing extension that has already been released to the public, we always start by copying the original folder and renaming it with the new version number. For example, the Horizontal Looper extension has gone through several revisions, starting with 1.0.0 and moving through 1.0.8 before changing functionality to support UltraDev 4 in versions 2.0.0 through 2.0.8 (micro versions that fixed bugs). ColdFusion data source support was added in 2.1.0 (a minor revision) and PHP support (another minor revision) in 2.2.0. This makes it easy to pinpoint the files and packages for each of the versions on the hard drive.

Deploying the Extension

In Chapter 6, we covered packaging an extension. An extension package serves several purposes:

▶ It allows you to bundle all of the files needed by your extension together in one place for transporting it.

▶ It allows for version control by giving the extension a version number that you can later update when you make changes in the package.

▶ It allows you to specify menu changes for extension organization.

▶ It allows for easy installation and removal.

▶ It allows you to distribute your extension to other people easily via e-mail or by posting the extension on a Web or FTP site.

You can use an extension by simply double-clicking the package and installing it to your machine. The files will be installed to the proper directories, and the menus will be updated to reflect the new extension. Other people can do the same with your extension, providing that the package is complete and they have the correct program to run it. For example, if you take advantage of the new features of Dreamweaver 4, you won't be able to deploy your extension to a machine that has Dreamweaver 3 on it. As long as your extension package is properly formatted with the correct information, the Extension Manager should take care of these details by prohibiting the extension from being installed unless the minimum requirements are met.

Your extensions might be for your own use only, or they might be for people who work within your company. Or, you may decide that you want the fame and glory that the extension developer receives and release your extensions for other Dreamweaver users. Whatever the reason for your foray into extension development, the extension package is the final product and should be treated as such. Just as a Christmas present is boxed, wrapped, and the little bow is finally placed on the package, the extension package should be complete, from the files and folders needed for the extension to run to the descriptive name placed on the final package. An extension with a meaningless name or a name that doesn't convey the functionality of the extension might never get used because its purpose is a mystery. A few simple rules should be followed for any extension that might be posted for public consumption:

▶ Don't overwrite Macromedia files in the extension. If you must make changes in a standard Dreamweaver file, make a copy of it under a different name and include it with your package.

▶   Don't overwrite files written by other people.

▶   If you include a reference to a shared file in an extension package file, make sure you reference it as shared. Otherwise, your extension will uninstall the file and cause other extensions to break.

▶   Use strict version control following the major.minor.micro convention. This makes it easier for bug control and also allows the Extension Manager to keep track of things more easily. It also lets people know which version they have and whether they need to upgrade. Keep in mind that you have to control the versioning on your shared files, as the Extension Manager can't tell the difference between two versions of one file.

▶   Use JavaScript comments liberally in the extension—for your own benefit as well as for the benefit of others who might use it. Two months from now, when you want to add a feature to your extension, you may forget why you originally wrote it the way you did.

▶   Include clear, concise instructions, either on the extension interface (if they are easy enough) or in a help file. The help file can be on a Web site or included in the package.

▶   Organize the extensions you write in a meaningful way. Don't just let them be appended to the bottom of a menu. Put your extensions in your own submenu.

If you follow a few simple guidelines, the entire extension writing process will become second nature, and you'll be able to create extensions more rapidly in an orderly fashion. In addition, if you are going to submit extensions to Macromedia, maintaining coding standards and following guidelines will make for a smoother submission process.

The Macromedia Exchange

The primary location for finding existing extensions and for uploading and sharing your own creations is the Macromedia Exchange. As of this writing, the Exchange is accepting extensions for Dreamweaver, UltraDev, Flash, and Fireworks. Anyone can upload a file to the Exchange for public consumption. Not only is it a place for sharing your work, it can also be a place to make a name for yourself or advertise your products and/or services. A popular extension could be downloaded 10,000–20,000 times or more, and it is a good way to get your name or your company's name into the minds of other Dreamweaver users.

The Exchange is located at **http://www.macromedia.com/exchange** and is extremely popular with Dreamweaver and other Macromedia product users. By providing an architecture that is easily expanded upon, Macromedia also opened the door to a thriving add-on market. The extension add-ons can be timesaving or production-enhancing commands, or they can be specific interfaces to your company's product. Some extensions even contain a login form that allows you to log in to your account with the extension creator accessing the information contained therein.

Downloading Extensions

To download or upload files, you have to first fill out a few simple forms and give yourself a username and password. Once you've done this, you are free to download and upload extensions to your heart's content. You don't have to sign in to download extensions—a cookie on your machine will give you access to the site. When uploading, however, you are required to sign in with your password. The Dreamweaver Exchange Welcome screen looks like this:

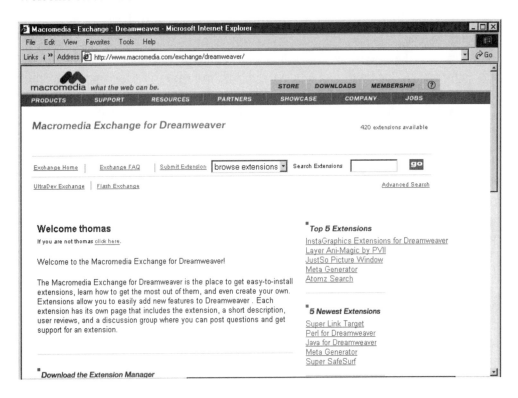

As you scroll down on the page, there is usually a list of the five featured extensions. These are generally extensions that are recent additions and stand out from other extensions in one way or another. Usually they are extensions that you don't want to be without, so it's always a good idea to start your downloads with these. There is also a select list that allows you to browse extensions by category:

Admittedly, these categories are sometimes misleading, and you can usually find things more easily by using the advanced search capabilities of the site. By clicking the advanced search link, you are taken to this page:

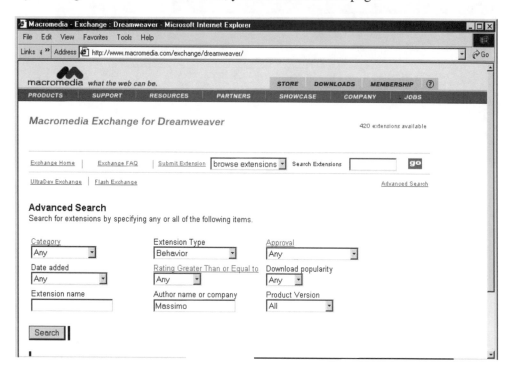

Here you can use the drop-down lists to narrow your search (such as searching for all extensions by Massimo), or you can search on a keyword, such as "CSS" or "Link," depending on what you're looking for. This is also a good place to look for extensions that you are thinking about writing. For example, before embarking on an object that writes e-mail links to the page, search on the Exchange for "Email link" to make sure you're not duplicating efforts.

Uploading Extensions

To upload an extension to the Exchange, you first need to login. You will then have to fill in a few simple pages of forms before you can upload your extension.

After logging in, the first page you come to will be a simple list of directions to follow:

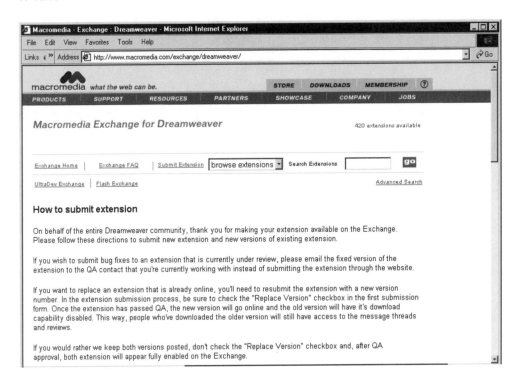

Next you are taken to Step One. This is the agreement between you and Macromedia. What you are basically doing here is accepting responsibility for your extension and granting Macromedia the right to house and distribute the extension on the Exchange for free. Read the requirements carefully—this step is like a contract between you and Macromedia:

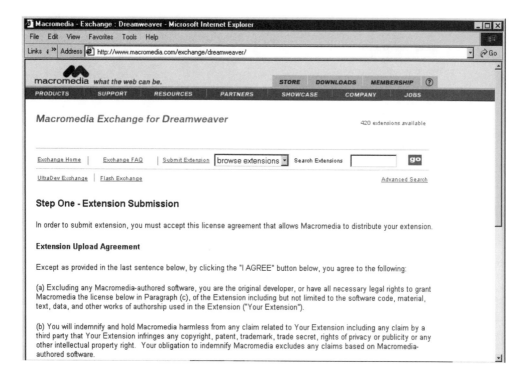

The next step is to upload the extension. When you get to this point, be aware that you should be committed to uploading the extension—if you bail out halfway through the process, the extension information will be in the Exchange database and you'll have to create a new version number to be able to upload the file on a future date (see the next illustration).

Next is the extension description. Most of this information comes right out of the MXI file, so it's up to you to make the description concise, readable, and descriptive. If this extension is replacing a previous version, you can note it here, and the old version will be removed when the new version is added. You can also check a box (not shown here) for Macromedia approval—extensions with a seal of approval from Macromedia conform to more strict standards:

Next is the personal stuff—your e-mail address, phone number (which is not posted and is for Macromedia internal use only), and contact information. Here is where you can also post a link to your Web site for a free plug on the Exchange:

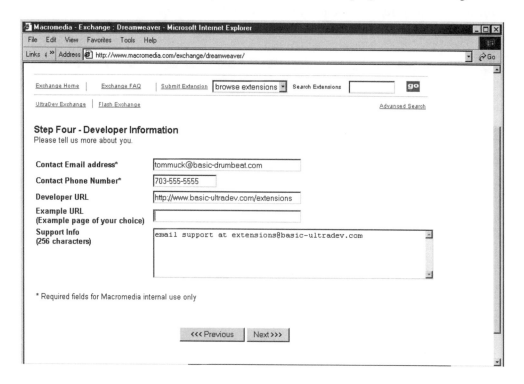

After clicking Next, you are taken to a verification screen where you can view the information one more time. After reviewing it, you can click Update to go back and make changes in the information, or you can choose to complete the submission process. If you go forward, you are taken to the final Thank You page, and the submission process is complete:

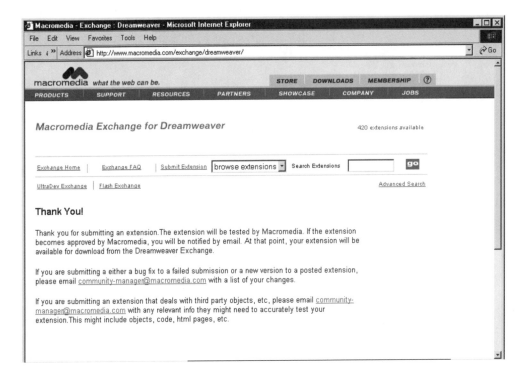

Once an extension is uploaded, it generally takes a few days for the Exchange QA managers to approve your extension. Macromedia approval generally takes a little longer, as there are stricter guidelines in place. The advantage to getting MM approval is that you have expert testing by the Macromedia QA engineers who will test your extension and give you bug reports. Once it is approved, it will appear in the Exchange and you'll soon be rich and famous. There are discussion groups for each extension, and a section for users to post comments and ratings.

Other Options

The Exchange is not the only place to upload extensions. You can also include them on your own Web site and track your own downloads. If you have a popular site, this can be a good way to get your extensions out there. For example, at **www.basic-ultradev.com** we have many of our own extensions available for download. There are also other Web sites that allow extensions to be uploaded, such as **www.UDZone.com**. On UDZone, you can upload your extensions and tutorials and monitor discussions of the extensions by having e-mail alerts sent to you when someone posts a new comment.

What to Take Away from this Book

Extension writing can be a rewarding experience. There's nothing better than building an extension that turns some complex task into a trivial one-click command and then seeing your new menu item become a part of the program that you use every day to build your Web pages. It's a satisfying experience that sometimes even overpowers the satisfaction involved in creating a Web site.

Extension writing can also be a little overwhelming to the beginner. This book is by no means an exhaustive approach to Dreamweaver and UltraDev extensions. It is intended to teach the budding extensionologist the basic principles and, we hope, to whet the appetite for delving deeper into the extensibility mechanism of Dreamweaver. Sometimes the manuals aren't enough—they are deep and cover a lot of territory, but they also require a basic understanding of Dreamweaver extensions before you can comprehend them. It's like diving into the deep end of the pool before knowing how to swim. You'll either drown or tire yourself out trying to stay afloat. In either case, you may not want to try it again. We hope this book will give you the enthusiasm you need to move forward in this fun and rewarding pastime.

Tom Muck and Ray West
June 2001

A

Shared Functions Reference

C hapter 1 covered some of the more popular API methods that are built into the Dreamweaver program. In addition to the JavaScript API, there are literally hundreds of useful functions contained in the Shared folder under the Configuration folder, among other places. The following sections take a look at just a few of the functions that are available in the Shared folder.

Shared CMN Folder Functions

This folder contains most of the shared functions that you will be using in your extensions. Most of the functions contained in this folder and the other folders are well documented inside each JavaScript file. Inline comments are often the best way to learn about the functions, but there are hundreds of functions. The brief overview that we're supplying here will help you determine where to look.

Shared\MM\Scripts\CMN\UI.js

This file contains functions to help with the user interface, including one of the most-used functions in extensionology, `findObject()`.

findObject(objName, parentObj)

The `findObject()` function replaces a lot of repetitive DOM accesses. When the OK button is clicked in your extension, your JavaScript code needs to fetch the values from the form that was just submitted. Suppose that you have a text field in your interface named recordset and a drop-down box named myOptionsBox. You could use:

```
var recordsetName = document.forms[0].recordset.value;
var myOptions =
document.forms[0].myOptionsBox.options[document.forms[0].
myOptionsBox.selectedIndex].text;
```

or use the `findObject()` function like this:

```
var recordsetName = findObject("recordset").value;
var myOptions =
findObject("myOptionsBox").options[findObject("myOptionsBox").
selectedIndex].text;
```

The first method uses the standard DOM methods of retrieving the object's properties, whereas the second method uses the findObject() function and is a little easier to read. The findObject() function returns the actual object that you are looking for, with all of the properties intact. You can make the reference to the drop-down select box even clearer and more easily understood by breaking the statement down into two statements:

```
var theBox = findObject("myOptionsBox");
var myOptions = theBox.options[theBox.selectedIndex].text;
```

This also solves the issue of referring to form elements inside layers using the Netscape 4 DOM that Dreamweaver uses. This function is absolutely essential when dealing with layers in your extensions.

wrapTextForAlert(*str, cols*)

This function should be self-explanatory—you can pass a string (*str*) and a maximum length (*cols*) to the function, and it will return the string with line breaks in the appropriate places. This is used to format a string for an alert box.

Shared\MM\Scripts\CMN\docInfo.js

This file has some helper functions for getting selected objects, creating names for elements, and a few other useful utility functions.

getAllObjectTags(tagName)

This function returns an array of all tags of the same type as the *tagName* attribute that you send to the function. For example, if you were looking for all tables on a page, you would call this function and assign the resulting array to a variable, such as the following:

```
var myTableTagArray = getAllObjectTags("table");
```

getSelectedObject()

This is a simple function that returns the object that is currently selected in the document, like this:

```
var theObject = getSelectedObject();
```

If you take a look at the actual function, it is pretty basic and illustrates another method of accessing an object. The entire function consists of two lines:

```
var currSel = dreamweaver.getSelection();
return dreamweaver.offsetsToNode(currSel[0],currSel[1]);
```

The first line gets the selection in the document made by the user, and the second line uses a built-in DOM method, offsetsToNode. This method converts the two offsets from the beginning of the document into the *node* that the selected code is contained within. In the following example

```
<table>
    <tr>
      <td>Hello</td>
    </tr>
</table>
```

if you highlight Hello in the document and pass the *offsets* (the number of characters into the document to the first character of the selection and the number of characters into the document to the first character after the selection) to the offsetsToNode built-in function, you are returned the object that contains the <td> tag set. You can test this using the following:

```
var test = getSelectedObject();
alert(test.outerHTML);
```

If you run this little scriptlet in an extension, an alert box pops up with <td>Hello</td> in it. So, while Hello is the selection, the selected object is the <td> node.

createUniqueName(tagName, tagString, arrToSearch)

You use this function if you are adding a tag for an object on the page and want the object to have a default name that is unique. Suppose your object inserts a check box on the page, but you want it to have a name such as checkbox2 because a checkbox1 already exists on the page. This function will do that for you.

The *tagName* variable is the tag that is being searched for. The *tagString* variable is the name that you want to use, such as *checkbox*, to return checkbox1 as your name. This name can be anything and doesn't have to match the default name for the tag in question. The *arrToSearch* variable is an optional array of elements to do the search in. If no array is given, the whole document is searched by default.

makeUniqueName(tag, baseName)

This function is similar to the last, except that you specify only a tag and a name. The function will create a unique name.

selectionInsideTag(tagName)

This function returns true or false, depending on whether the currently selected text is within a particular tag. Suppose your extension depends on the selection being within a table cell. You could access this function as follows:

```
if (selectionInsideTag("td")) {
//it is!  do something with it
} else {
//it's not.  Error condition
};
```

isUltraDev()

This function tells you whether the current application is UltraDev. It returns true if the application is UltraDev.

Shared\MM\Scripts\CMN\DOM.js

The file contains some functions that deal specifically with the Dreamweaver DOM and make the process of finding nodes and tags easier within the DOM. The DOM.js file also contains several functions that help with the updating of Behaviors and Behavior functions on the page.

findTag(tagName)

This function returns a node containing the object of a specific tag you are looking for. You can also pass it a *startNode* variable as the second element in the *tagName* array. This is an optional variable, and if it isn't given, the function will search the entire document.

nodeList(startNode)

This function returns an array of all nodes that are within a node passed to the function. If, for example, you pass it the node consisting of the following text:

```
<table><tr><td>hello</td></tr></table>
```

the result returned will be a three-element array with the <table> node, the <tr> node, and the <td> node.

getRootNode()

This is a simple one-line function that returns the root node of the document.

traverse(node, fElementHandler)

If you pass a node to this function, it will traverse the entire DOM structure, calling a handler (callback) function for each node type that it encounters. Optional arguments are fTextHandler, fCommentHandler, and userData.

isInsideTag(tag, tagNames)

This function is passed to two parameters: the tag name you are searching for and the list of tags in which to search for it. The *tagNames* variable is a comma-separated list of tags that you want to check for the existence of a specific tag name. For instance, if you want to see whether there is a <b> tag within any heading tags, you can call the function like this:

```
if (isInsideTag("b","h1,h2,h3,h4,h5,h6")) {
//it is--do something
} else {
//it isn't--do something else
};
```

getSelectionLink()

This function checks to see if the selection or any parent of the selection is a link and returns the link node if found.

Behavior Functions

These functions allow you to update Behaviors and Behavior functions that are on a page. The updateBehaviorFns() updates all Behavior functions on the page and calls a couple other utility functions that are also in this file: getFunctionVersion(fnName, dom) and deleteFunction(fnName, dom). In addition to these Behavior helper functions, there are a few others that you should look at if you plan to do a lot of work with behaviors: deleteFunctionCall(fnName, dom), hasFunctionCall(fnName, dom), and scriptIsEmpty(aScript).

Shared\MM\Scripts\CMN\file.js

This file contains several functions to make it easier to deal with files and file path URLs.

browseFile(fieldToStoreURL)

With this function, you pass a text field name into the *fieldToStoreURL* variable. Typically, you invoke this function with a button or an image of a small folder next to the text field that you want to store the filename in. Then you can call it in the onClick event of that button or image field. It brings up the Select File dialog box and inserts the result into the text field:

```
<input type="text" name="myTextField">
<input type="button" value="Browse..."
 onclick="browseFile('myTextField') ">
```

getFullPath(filePathURL)

This function converts doc-relative, site-relative, or absolute file paths into full paths that start with file:// so that DWfile can use the path and deal with the file properly.

getSimpleFileName()

This function will return the filename of the current document only. It will look at the current document and get its full path and then strip off the extraneous path information.

fixUpPath(docURL, siteURL, savedPath)

This function is used to return a path that depends on the current status of the document. If you pass to this function the location of the current document, the site root, and the path to a file or folder (expressed as a file://*URL*), it will return one of the following:

▶ If the document has not been saved, it returns the file://*URL* that was passed in.

▶ If the document is not in the current site, it returns the file://*URL* that was passed in.

▶ If the document has been saved in the current site, it returns a document-relative path.

fileIsCurrentlyOpen(absoluteFilePath)

You can pass a file path to this function and it will tell you if the file is currently open.

Shared\MM\Scripts\CMN\form.js

This file contains only a few functions, but they are very handy if you are writing extensions that deal with forms or form objects.

IPIsInsideOfForm()

This function returns true or false depending on whether the cursor is currently inside a form. If the cursor is contained in a layer, the function will only search within the layer because you can't split a form tag across layers.

> **NOTE**
>
> When referring to layers in the Dreamweaver environment, the term generally refers to `<div>`, `<span>`, `<layer>`, and `<ilayer>` tags.

checkForFormTag(formItemStr)

This function is handy if you happen to be inserting a form element, such as a special-purpose text field or check box that you've designed. Simply pass the string containing the HTML that you are putting on the page, and the function will check to see whether the text will be contained within a form tag after it gets inserted. It does this by checking the currently selected text and looking up the tree until it finds a form tag. If there is no form tag, the function will put a form tag around your text and make sure it has a unique name. If your selection is contained within a layer, the function will only search within the layer because a form tag can't be split across layers.

isLayer(obj)

When passed an object (node), this function indicates whether or not the given object is a layer by checking for all possible layer tags—`<layer>`, `<ilayer>`, `<div>`, and `<span>`.

Shared\MM\Scripts\CMN\insertion.js

This file contains only a few functions, but the `insertIntoDocument()` function can be quite handy for inserting code into a document.

insertIntoDocument(textStr, bBlockTag)

This function inserts a string of text into a document, plain and simple. The text can be anything—HTML, text, or JavaScript. Simply pass the text you want inserted at the insertion point to the function using the *textStr* variable and set the bBlockTag argument to true if the text you are inserting is a block-level tag, such as a layer, table, heading, or form. You set the bBlockTag to true because the function will close off any open block-level tag before inserting the code, such as when there is an open <p> tag. The function will generate a closing </p> tag in front of your code and reopen it immediately after the code that is inserted. This function is generally used by extensions other than Objects. The built-in function called objectTag() is used in Objects to automatically insert your text.

arrContains(arr, itemToFind)

This function is a shortcut method to find a given string in an array. Simply pass to the function the array and the string to be found, and it will return true if the array contains the string.

Shared\MM\Scripts\CMN\string.js

This file contains a wealth of functions that make it easy to deal with strings. If you have any sort of string formatting to do, look at this file. Only a few of the functions are listed here.

badChars(theStr)

Pass any string to this function and it will tell you whether the string contains one of the following bad characters:

```
~!@#$%^&*()_+|`-=\{}[]:";'<>,./?
```

The function returns true if any of these characters are in the string.

getParam(tagStr, param)

This function returns the value of any named parameter from a string passed to it. In the example <cfquery name="recordset1">, *tagStr* is equal to <cfquery name="recordset1"> and *name* is the parameter. The function will return an array with recordset1 being element [0] in the array. Suppose you pass the following string:

```
var myString = '<TD><IMG SRC="trans.gif" Align="left" Width="1"
Height="1"></TD>'
using this expression:

var myWidth =  getParam(theString, "Width");
```

The function would return "1" as *myWidth*.

quote(textStr, quoteType)

This function simply wraps the *textStr* variable that is passed to the function in single or double quotes, depending on the value of *quoteType*. Use 1 for single quotes and 2 for double quotes.

stripSpaces(theStr)

This function strips the leading and trailing spaces off a string that is passed to it.

AllInRange(x,y,theString)

This function returns true if all characters in *theString* fall in the range of characters *x* and *y* (inclusive). For example, if you pass a string like "1234" to the function with *x* and *y* values of "1" and "5", the function would return true because the numbers are within the given range. The values are compared as strings, so "a" would be less than "b".

reformat (s)

This is a handy function for reformatting strings to a given pattern. The function takes as arguments the string you are reformatting followed by alternating numbers and strings for the reformat. The number specifies how many characters of the string to add to the newly reformatted string, and designates the following string to be the next divider in the newly reformatted string. For example, if you pass this to the function:

```
var myZipCode = reformat("220317323",5, "-")
```

the variable *myZipCode* would now contain the string "22031-7323". For another example, suppose you want to reformat a phone number. You could call the function like this:

```
var myPhoneNumber = reformat("7035553434", 0, "(", 3, ") ", 3, "-")
```

After calling the function, the string that is returned to the *myPhoneNumber* variable would be "(703) 555-3434".

Shared Class Folder

This folder contains several useful classes that make it easy to deal with some of the complex JavaScript functionality of the Dreamweaver DOM. One very popular class is the ListControlClass, located in this folder. Classes often hide the intricacies of the object from the user and make it easier to use the various methods of the object. In the case of the ListControlClass, for example, it's much easier to refer to `myList.get()` rather than `document.forms[0].myList.options[document.forms[0].myList.selectedIndex].text`. Other class files contained in this folder are as follows:

- ▶ **classCheckbox.js**   Turns the standard check box into an easily manipulated class.

- ▶ **FileClass.js**   Makes handling files and file paths much easier.

- ▶ **GridClass.js**   Used for the MM:TREECONTROL that is unique to Dreamweaver and UltraDev.

- ▶ **GridControlClass.js**   Used for a Grid Control.

- ▶ **ImageButtonClass.js**   Allows you to use an image input form element as a special image button class.

- ▶ **NameValuePairClass.js**   Creates and manages a list of name/value pairs.

- ▶ **TabControlClass.js**   Used to make multitabbed extension interfaces.

- ▶ **PageControlClass.js**   Used by the TabControlClass.

- ▶ **PreferencesClass.js**   Makes it easy to store preferences for a command.

- ▶ **RadioGroupClass.js**   Turns the standard radio button into an easily manipulated class.

UltraDev Shared Files

UltraDev has a special folder under the Shared directory that has most of the server-side extension functionality. Much can be learned about the UltraDev extensibility mechanism just by going through all of the files in this directory and learning how some of the common functions in this folder work.

- ▶ **dataSourceCmn.js**   Contains much of the functionality for Data Sources, including the ObjectInfo. ObjectInfo is the return structure for the `findDynamicSources()` and `generateDynamicSourceBindings()` functions in a data source file. If you plan to do any data source extensions, you should be thoroughly familiar with this file.

▶ **DBTreeControlClass.js** Creates the DBTreeControlClass used in the recordset. You can use this control in your own extensions as well.

▶ **dynamicCmn.js** Used by dynamic server-side data sources.

▶ **parseSimpleSQL.js** Used by UltraDev to parse SQL statements entered in the Recordset dialog box.

▶ **PlusMinusButton.js** A simple class used by the plus (+) and minus (−) buttons in the extension interface.

▶ **ReplaceChunks.js** Contains a few useful functions for replacing sections of code in an UltraDev file.

▶ **ReservedWords.js** Contains one function, `isReservedWord()`, and a list of reserved words in the UltraDev environment. You can use this if you want to verify user input or variables used in extension writing.

▶ **sbManager.js** One of the main files that give UltraDev its functionality; the Server Behaviors use this file for management.

▶ **SchemaCache.js** Cache management in UltraDev for cached recordsets and stored procedures.

▶ **SQLTypes.js** Contains functions that are aids in determining database column types.

▶ **ssClasses.js** Contains definitions of two of the main Server Behavior classes: ssRecord and ssEdits. This file should be studied if you plan to do any serious work in UltraDev.

▶ **ssCmnElements.js** Contains many of the common functions used in UltraDev Server Behaviors, such as findAllRecordsetNames().

▶ **ssDocManager.js** Contains core UD functionality that helps with the insertion of server side code.

▶ **TempURL.js** Allows UltraDev to store design note information about temporary files.

Other Important Files

We've discussed many of the types of extensions that are available to the Dreamweaver programmer, but there are some other files that don't fall into any specific category, other than "you have to know about these." We'll discuss a few of them here.

Extensions.txt

This file is found in the root of the Configuration folder. It is a text file that lists file extensions used by Dreamweaver, but it's extensible as well. This file contains the three- and four-letter file extensions that pop up in the Open and Save dialog boxes inside the Dreamweaver environment. For example, if you work with your own file type with the three-letter extension .bud, you could place that in this file and it would always show up as one of the choices when you open or save a document.

SourceFormat.txt

This text document contains user preferences for how the HTML should be formatted, such as the autowrap, upper- or lowercase tags, and so on. It also has specific information about each tag so that when you apply the Format Source command, the instructions in this file will be maintained. Each tag is listed with indentation levels and line break instructions, in the format of

```
<tag break="[before], [inside start], [inside end], [after]"
[optional attributes]>
```

The optional attributes are:

- ▶ **INDENT**   Indents the contents
- ▶ **IGROUP = "indention group number" (1 through 8)**   Indents grouping level
- ▶ **NAMECASE = "CustomName"**   Specific name case
- ▶ **NOFORMAT**   Prevents formatting on this tag

For example, the `<center>` tag is listed like this:

```
<center break="1,1,1,1" indent>
```

The line breaks occur before the tag, inside the start tag, inside the end tag, and after the end tag. If you apply center tags somewhere in your page and apply source formatting, the line breaks will all be inserted at the appropriate locations. In addition, it is specified that the contents of the tag should be indented.

TagAttributeList.txt

This is a list of attributes used by the Quick Tag Editor, Search Dialog, and Property Inspectors. It contains lists of the various attributes of all tags used in Dreamweaver. If you add your own tag to Dreamweaver, you may want to modify this file as well.

localTextDW.htm and localTextUltraDev.htm

The Startup folder contains a few useful files that are run every time Dreamweaver starts up. You can consider putting a file in here if there is anything that you need to do as the program starts up, such as initialize a global variable. The localTextDW.htm file, for example, contains a list of many of the global error messages that pop up at various times in alert boxes. How often have you seen in an extension alert (MM.MSG_InvalidName) or something similar? Command files frequently contain references to global button names, such as MM.BTN_OK or MM.BTN_Cancel. These are all in this file.

The localTextUltraDev.htm file is similar, but it contains many more global variables that are used in the UltraDev program.

Summary

These are just some of the functions and files available. As you develop new extensions and rework existing extensions, you will find yourself doing some tasks over and over. The functions contained within the Shared folder are tested and used by Dreamweaver and UltraDev and can greatly reduce the amount of code you have to write. You have to figure that if there is something you need to do in an extension, someone has probably done something similar in the past. Also, as you write functions that you might need to reuse, you can package them with your extensions and place your own folder in the Shared folder.

lthough this is the first book dedicated to writing extensions, there are some other handy references that you may want to look into that will help you during the extension writing process.

Web Sites

One of the best ways to learn how to develop extensions is to look at extensions written by others. Here are a few useful links to extensions, as well as some other good sites that are relevant to the extension writer.

http://www.basic-ultradev.com   Our site. Many extensions available, plus a few tutorials for extension writers.

http://www.massimocorner.com   Massimo Foti's corner of the Web has tons of extensions for Dreamweaver and UltraDev.

http://www.publicdomain.co.uk   Awesome extensions that push the limits of Dreamweaver extensibility.

http://www.udzone.com   UltraDev extensions and related topics from George Petrov and Waldo Smeets. Great extensions, tutorials, and community site.

http://www.projectseven.com   Al Sparber's Dreamweaver and UltraDev tutorials, extensions, and design packs.

http://www.macromedia.com/support/dreamweaver/extend/form/   Macromedia's UltraDev and Dreamweaver extensibility newsgroup.

http://www.extending-dreamweaver.com   Stefan van As, creator of the Script Inspector for Dreamweaver, runs this site, which is devoted to DW extensions.

http://www.macromedia.com/exchange/dreamweaver/   The Exchange is the prime place to find extensions.

http://www.yaromat.com   Jaro von Flocken's site with some popular extensions.

http://hotwired.lycos.com/webmonkey/99/11/index2a.html   Webmonkey's original Extending Dreamweaver tutorial.

http://www.macromedia.com/support/ultradev/behaviors/create_extensions/   Original Macromedia document for creating Server Behaviors in ten easy steps.

news://forums.macromedia.com   Macromedia has support forums for all of their programs, as well as the Exchange. Check them out in your newsreader and become a member of the community.

Books

The Extending Dreamweaver and UltraDev book is available directly from Macromedia at a low price that covers printing. At over 700 pages, it is a must have for the extension developer. It is identical to the Extending Dreamweaver help files that are installed by default with Dreamweaver and UltraDev, but it's much handier to have in printed form. You can find it at the Macromedia Web site at www.macromedia.com. Other books that you may want to have on your shelf include the following:

Dreamweaver Ultradev 4: The Complete Reference

by Ray West, Tom Muck, and Tom Allen
Paperback, 834 pages (February 2001)
Osborne McGraw-Hill
ISBN: 0072130172

We're a little biased because we wrote the book, but it's currently the best source for anyone wishing to delve into UltraDev extensions—180 pages devoted to extension writing.

Javascript Bible, 4th Edition

by Danny Goodman
Paperback, 1104 pages (March 2001)
Hungry Minds, Inc.
ISBN: 0764533428

Every extension writer needs a JavaScript reference. If you are just starting out, this book is a good overview as well as a good reference.

Javascript: The Definitive Guide, 3rd edition

by David Flanagan
Paperback, 776 pages (June 1998)
O'Reilly & Associates
ISBN: 1565923928

This book is probably the best introduction to JavaScript, with a good section about regular expressions.

Pure Javascript

by R. Allen Wyke, Charlton Ting, and Jason Gilliam
Paperback, 1448 pages (June 1999)
Sams
ISBN: 0672315475

This book is the definitive reference for JavaScript. Not good if you want to learn JavaScript, but a must to have on your shelf for looking up any JavaScript function.

JavaScript Programmer's Reference

by Cliff Wootton
Paperback, 1000 pages (February 2001)
Wrox Press, Inc.
ISBN: 1861004591

At least as good as the Pure JavaScript reference is the JavaScript Programmer's Reference from Wrox, which is newer and covers the latest DOM. A dedicated extensionologist will have both on his shelf.

XML Bible

by Elliotte Rusty Harold
Paperback, 1015 pages (July 1999)
IDG Books Worldwide
ISBN: 0764532367

The XML contained in Dreamweaver and UltraDev isn't true XML, but you should have at least one XML book in your library to be able to better understand the underlying architecture of XML.

Mastering Regular Expressions

by Jeffrey E. Friedl
Paperback, 368 pages (January 1997)
O'Reilly & Associates
ISBN: 1565922573

Regular expressions are a big part of Dreamweaver extension writing and a must if you want to write UltraDev extensions. This book isn't about JavaScript regular expressions, but all of the techniques and examples apply to them.

Dreamweaver 4 Bible

by Joseph W. Lowery
Paperback, 1100 pages (May 2001)
Hungry Minds, Inc.
ISBN: 0764535692

Several chapters on building Dreamweaver extensions by one of the top names in the Dreamweaver community.

Dreamweaver 4 Developer's Guide

by Drew McLellan
Paperback, 604 pages (May 2001)
McGraw-Hill Professional
ISBN: 0072132280

Drew has quickly made a name for himself in the Dreamweaver community as one of the top experts. This book is an advanced look at Dreamweaver and has a large amount of information available about Dreamweaver extension writing.

Index

INTERNATIONAL CONTACT INFORMATION

AUSTRALIA
McGraw-Hill Book Company Australia Pty. Ltd.
TEL +61-2-9417-9899
FAX +61-2-9417-5687
http://www.mcgraw-hill.com.au
books-it_sydney@mcgraw-hill.com

CANADA
McGraw-Hill Ryerson Ltd.
TEL +905-430-5000
FAX +905-430-5020
http://www.mcgrawhill.ca

GREECE, MIDDLE EAST,
NORTHERN AFRICA
McGraw-Hill Hellas
TEL +30-1-656-0990-3-4
FAX +30-1-654-5525

MEXICO (Also serving Latin America)
McGraw-Hill Interamericana Editores S.A. de C.V.
TEL +525-117-1583
FAX +525-117-1589
http://www.mcgraw-hill.com.mx
fernando_castellanos@mcgraw-hill.com

SINGAPORE (Serving Asia)
McGraw-Hill Book Company
TEL +65-863-1580
FAX +65-862-3354
http://www.mcgraw-hill.com.sg
mghasia@mcgraw-hill.com

SOUTH AFRICA
McGraw-Hill South Africa
TEL +27-11-622-7512
FAX +27-11-622-9045
robyn_swanepoel@mcgraw-hill.com

UNITED KINGDOM & EUROPE
(Excluding Southern Europe)
McGraw-Hill Education Europe
TEL +44-1-628-502500
FAX +44-1-628-770224
http://www.mcgraw-hill.co.uk
computing_neurope@mcgraw-hill.com

ALL OTHER INQUIRIES Contact:
Osborne/McGraw-Hill
TEL +1-510-549-6600
FAX +1-510-883-7600
http://www.osborne.com
omg_international@mcgraw-hill.com